Git

Distributed Version Control Fundamentals and Workflows

René Preißel & Bjørn Stachmann

Git: Distributed Version Control – Fundamentals and Workflows
Original Title: Dezentrale Versionsverwaltung im Team - Grundlagen und Workflows

Original ISBN: 978-3-86490-130-0

First Edition: October 2014

ISBN: 978-1-77197-000-6

Printed in the United States of America
Book and Cover Designer: Brainy Software Team

Technical Reviewer: Budi Kurniawan
Indexer: Chris Mayle

Trademarks

Warning and Disclaimer

Table of Contents

Introduction

Welcome to *Git: Distributed Version Control – Fundamentals and Workflows*.

In this introduction, you will find what Git can do for you and why you need this book.

Why Git?

Git has a tremendous success story behind it. In April 2005, Linus Torvalds began to implement Git because he did not like any of the open-source version control systems available at that time.

Today, searching for "git version control" on Google returns millions of results. Git has almost become a standard for new open-source projects. Many large open source projects have already been migrated to Git or are about to be.

Here are some of the reasons why so many people are choosing Git.

- **Git allows you to work with branches:** In a project where many developers work in parallel, there will be many different lines of development. The strength of Git lies in the tools that can help development strands re-integrate: merging, rebasing, cherry-picking, etc.
- **Flexibility in the workflow:** Git is exceptionally flexible. A single developer can use it, an agile team will find ways to work with it and even a large

international project with numerous developers at multiple sites can develop a good workflow with it.

- **Contribution:** Most open source projects exist through voluntary contributions from developers. It is important to make the process of contributing as simple as possible. With a centralized version control system, this is often difficult because you do not want to give everyone write access to the repository. With Git, anyone can clone a repository, work independently and later pass the changes around.
- **Performance:** Git is still fast even when handling a project with many files and a long history. For example, Git can switch the current version of Linux kernel sources to a six-year older version in less than a minute on a Macbook Air. This is impressive considering there are over 200,000 commits and 40,000 changed files between the two versions.
- **Robust against failures and attacks:** Since the project history is spread over a number of distributed repositories, a serious loss of data is unlikely. An ingeniously simple data structure in the repository ensures that data will still be interpreted correctly in the distant future. The consistent use of cryptographic checksums makes it difficult for attackers to tamper with a repository unnoticed.
- **Offline and multi-site development:** The distributed architecture makes it easy to develop offline or when traveling. In multi-site development, neither a central server nor a permanent network connection is required.
- **Strong open source community:** In addition to detailed official documentation, there are numerous manuals, forums, wikis, etc. There is an ecosystem of tools, hosting platforms, publications, services and plug-ins for development environments, and it is growing healthily.
- **Expandability:** Git offers convenient commands for the user, including commands that allow for more

direct access to the repository. This makes Git very flexible and allows individual applications to have more than what the default version of Git offers.

A Book for Professional Developers

If you are a developer working in a team and wanting to know how to use Git effectively, then you are holding the right book. This book is not a theory-heavy tome or a comprehensive reference. It does not explain all the commands in Git (there are more than 100) or all the options (some commands have over 50 options). Instead, this book teaches you how to use Git in typical project environments, such as how to set up a Git project and how to create a Git release.

About This Book

Here is what you can expect from this book.

- **Getting Started:** Shows an example of every important Git command in less than a dozen pages.
- **Introduction:** In not more than a hundred pages you will learn everything you need to work with Git in a team. A large number of examples show how to use the main Git commands. Furthermore, basic concepts, such as commit, repository, branch, merge and rebase, are explained to help you understand how Git works. You will also find a section containing tips and tricks that you probably do not need every day, but which sometimes can be useful.
- **Workflows:** Workflows describe scenarios where you can use Git in a project, such as when you want to create a release. For each workflow the following is explained so that the desired results can be achieved:

- what problem it solves,
- what conditions must be added, and
- who has to do what and when it has to be done.
- **"Why This Solution?" sections:** Each workflow describes exactly one concrete solution. In Git, there are often very different paths that you can take to achieve the same goal. In the last part of each workflow chapter we explain why we have chosen exactly this solution. We will mention if there are variations and alternatives that might be of interest to you.
- **"Step by Step" instructions:** Frequently used command sequences, such as moving a branch, are given in "Step by Step" instructions.

Why Workflows?

Git is extremely flexible. It can be used by many in different roles, from a single system admin who needs to version a few shell scripts occasionally, to the hundreds of developers in the Linux kernel project. Anything is possible. However, this flexibility comes at a price. Before you start working with Git, you have to make a number of decisions. For example:

- In Git you have distributed repositories. However, will you really only work locally? Or will you prefer to set up a central repository?
- Git supports two types of data transfer: push and pull. Should you use both? If you choose one, which one? Why not the other?
- Branching and merging are two of the features Git is strong in. But how many branches should you open? One for each software feature? One for each release? Or just one?

To get you started, we have summarized what workflows are or do:

- Workflows are procedures for everyday project work.
- Workflows give specific instructions.
- Workflows show the necessary commands and options.
- Workflows are well suited for teams who are working closely, as those in modern software projects often are.
- Some workflows are not the only right solution for the problem, but are a good starting point from which you can develop efficient workflows for your project.

We focus on agile development teams working on commercial projects, because we believe that many professional developers (including the authors) are working in such environments. Not included are special requirements that are suited for large projects because they have significantly inflated workflows and because we believe that they are not that interesting to most developers. Also not included is the open source development, although there is a very interesting workflow with Git for this.

Tips for the Reader

As authors we obviously want you to read our book from cover to cover. But, let's face it: Do you have time to even read more than a few pages? We suspect your project is still ongoing and that working with Git is only one of a hundred issues that you are dealing with at this moment. Therefore, we have made every effort to write a book that people can skim over. Here are a few things to consider:

Do I have to read the introductory chapters to understand the workflows?

If you have no previous knowledge of Git, then yes. You need to master the basic commands and principles to be able to use the workflows correctly.

I have worked with Git. Which chapters can I skip?

There is a summary on the last page of every introductory chapter (Chapters 1 to 11). Here you can read very quickly to figure out if there are still things new to you in the chapter or if you can skip the whole chapter. The following are chapters you can safely skip because they are only relevant for some workflows:

- Chapter 5, "The Repository"
- Chapter 8, "A Cleaner History with Rebasing"
- Chapter 10, "Version Tagging"
- Chapter 11, "Dependencies between Repositories"

Where Can I Find It?

- Step by Step instructions.
- Commands and options: If you want to know, for example, what a command does and what options can be used with it, see the Index. Almost all commands and options are listed there.
- Technical terms: Naturally, all terms in this book can be found in the Index.

Examples and Notations

We use the command line in many examples in this book. This does not mean there is no graphical user interfaces for Git. In fact, there are already two graphical user interface

(GUI) applications for Git. In addition, there are numerous Git front-ends, including the following.

- Atlassian SourceTree (http://www.sourcetreeapp.com)
- TortoiseGit (http://code.google.com/p/tortoisegit)
- SmartGit (http://www.syntevo.com/smartgit)
- GitX (http://gitx.frim.nl)
- Git Extensions (http://code.google.com/p/gitextensions)
- tig (http://jonas.nitro.dk/tig)
- qgit (http://sourceforge.net/projects/qgit)
- Git in development environments that support Git internally, such as IntelliJ8 (http://www.jetbrains.com/idea) and Xcode 4 (http://developer.apple.com/technologies/tools)
- Git plug-ins for integrated development environments, such as Egit for Eclipse (http://eclipse.org/egit), NBGit for NetBeans (http://nbgit.org), Git Extensions for Visual STUDIO (http://code.google.com/p/gitextensions)

In spite of this, we have decided to use the command line in the examples because

- Git command line commands work on all platforms,
- the examples will work with future versions of Git,
- they thus represent very compact workflows,
- we believe that working with the command line is most efficient for many applications.

In the examples we use the standard bash shell on Linux and Mac OS systems. On Windows you can use the "Git Bash" shell (included in msysgit, a Git application for Windows that can be downloaded from http://msysgit.github.io) or cygwin.

A command line call looks like this.

```
> git commit
```

Where interesting, we also show the response from Git, e.g.

```
> git --version
git version 1.8.3.4
```

Acknowledgments

Looking back, we are amazed at how many people have contributed to the creation of this book in one or the other way. We would like to thank all those without whom this book would not have been what it is now.

First of all we would like to thank Anke, Jan, Elke and Annika, who now barely remember what we look like without a laptop under our fingers.

We would also like to thank the friendly team at dpunkt Publishing, the publisher of the original (German) edition of this book, especially Vanessa Wittmer, Nadine Thiele and Ursula Zimpfer. Special thanks to René Schonfeldt, Maurice Kowalski, Jochen Schlosser, Oliver Zeigermann, Ralf Degner, Michael Schulze-Ruhfus, and half a dozen anonymous reviewers for their valuable feedback that helped make this book better.

Standing on the Shoulders of Giants

A special thanks to Linus Torvalds, Junio C. Hamano and the many committers of the Git project. They have given the developer community this fantastic tool.

Chapter 1
Basic Concepts

This chapter introduces you to the idea of a distributed version control system and shows you how it differs from a centralized one. In this chapter you will also learn how distributed repositories work and why branching and merging are not a big deal in Git.

Distributed Version Control, How Different?

Before looking into the concepts of distributed version control, let's take a quick look at the classic architecture of centralized version control.

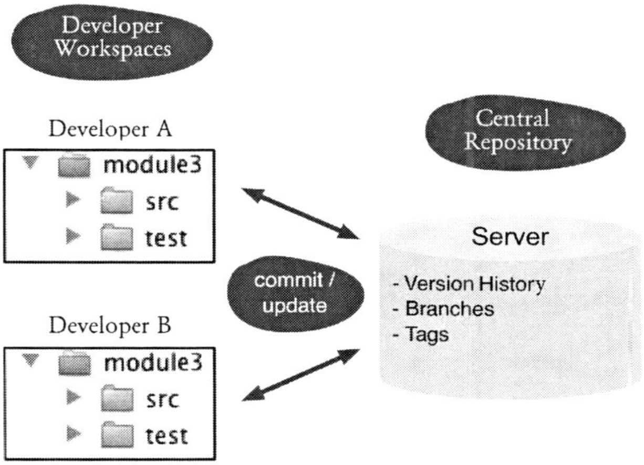

Figure 1.1: Centralized version control

Figure 1.1 shows the typical layout of a centralized version control system, such as CVS or Subversion. Every developer has a working directory (workspace) with all the project files in his or her computer. After the developer makes changes locally, he or she then sends the changes by regularly committing to a central server. With an update the developer retrieves changes made by other developers. The central server stores the current and historical versions of files (repository). Parallel development branches and named versions (tags) are also managed centrally.

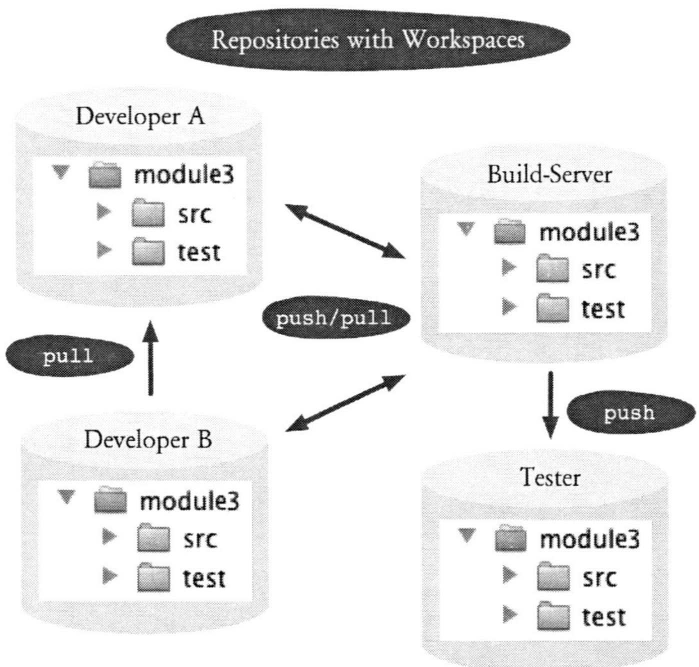

Figure 1.2: Distributed version control

In a distributed version control system (see Figure 1.2) there is no separation between the developer environment and the server environment. Every developer has both a workspace with the files being worked on and their own local repository (called a clone) with all versions, branches and tags. Changes are also enshrined here with a commit, but initially only in the local repository. Other developers see the new versions immediately. Push and pull commands then transmit changes from one repository to another. Technically, all repositories are equivalent in the distributed architecture. In theory, it does not need a server: You could transfer all changes directly from one development computer to another development computer. In practice server repositories play an important role in Git, for example in the form of the following specific repositories:

- **Blessed repository:** In this repository, "official" releases are created.
- **Shared repository:** This repository is used to exchange files between developers in the team. In a small project, the blessed repository can be used for this purpose. In multi-site development, there may be several of these repositories.
- **Workflow repository:** A workflow repository is filled only with changes that have achieved a certain status in the workflow, such as after a successful review.
- **Fork repository:** This repository is used to decouple from the development main line (for example, for large conversions that do not fit in the normal release cycle) or for experimental developments that may never be included in the main line.

Here are the advantages of a distributed system over a centralized one.

- **High performance:** Almost all operations are performed locally without network access.
- **Efficient ways of working:** Developers can use local branches to quickly switch between different tasks.
- **Offline capability:** Developers can perform commits, create branches, tag versions, etc. without a server connection. They can upload them later.

- **Flexible development processes:** In teams and companies specialized repositories can be created in order to communicate with other departments, such as the testers. Changes are easily released with a push into this repository.
- **Backup:** Every developer has a copy of the repository with a full history. Thus, the probability of losing data due to server failure is slim.
- **Maintainability:** Tricky restructuring can first be tried on a copy of a repository before being transmitted to the original repository.

The Repository, the Basis of Distributed Work

The repository is basically an efficient data storage. In a nutshell, it contains:

- **Files (blobs):** These contain text or binary data. The data will be saved regardless of the file name.
- **Directories (Trees):** Directories associate file names with content. Directories can in turn contain other directories.
- **Versions (commits):** A version defines a recoverable state of a directory. When creating a new version, the author, the time, a comment and the previous version will be stored.

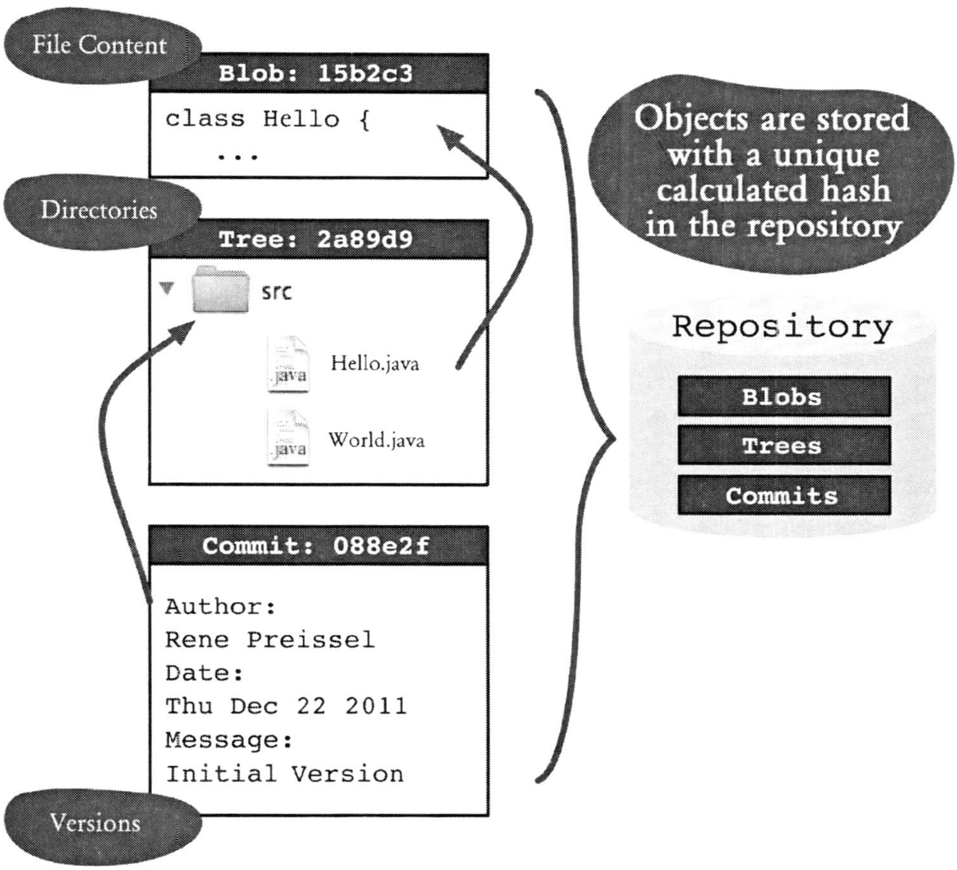

Figure 1.3: Storage of objects in the repository

For all data a hexadecimal hash is calculated, eg 1632acb65b01c6b621d6e1105205773931bb1a41. This hash is used as reference between the objects and as a key to recover the data later (See Figure 1.3).

The hash of a commit is its "version number." If you have a commit hash, you can check if this version is included in a repository and you can restore the associated directory in the workspace. If the version is not available, you can import (pull) that commit along with all the referenced objects from another repository.

The following are the advantages of using the hash and the given repository structure:

- **High Performance:** Access to data via the hash is very fast.
- **Redundancy-free storage:** Identical file content needs to be stored only once.
- **Distributed version numbers:** Because the hash of the files, the author and the date is calculated, versions can also be generated "offline" without causing conflicts in the future.
- **Efficient synchronization between repositories:** When a commit from one repository to another is transferred, only objects that do not yet exist will be copied. Figuring out whether an object already exists is very fast thanks to the hash.
- **Data integrity:** The hash is calculated from the content of the data. You can check with Git any time if a hash matches the data. Unintentional changes or malicious manipulation of data can be detected.
- **Automatic rename detection:** Renamed files are automatically detected since the hash of the content does not change. Therefore, no special commands for renaming and moving are necessary.

Branching and Merging, Easy!

For the majority of version control systems, branching and merging are exceptional circumstances that are considered advanced topics. Git, on the other hand, was originally created for Linux kernel developers who were scattered all over the world. Merging of many individual results had been one of the biggest challenges, so one of the design objectives of Git was to make branching and merging as easy and safe as possible.

Figure 1.4 shows how developers working in parallel cause branches to be created. Each point represents a version (commit) of the project. In Git you can only version the entire project, and thus each point represents files that belong to the same version.

Both developers start with the same version. After both of them make changes, they commit their changes. As each of the developers has his/her own repository, now there are two different versions of the project: two branches have been created. If one of the developers imports the changes from the other developer, he/she can make Git merge the versions. If the merge is successful, Git will create a merge commit, which include changes from both developers. If the other developer picks this commit, both developers will again have the same version of the project.

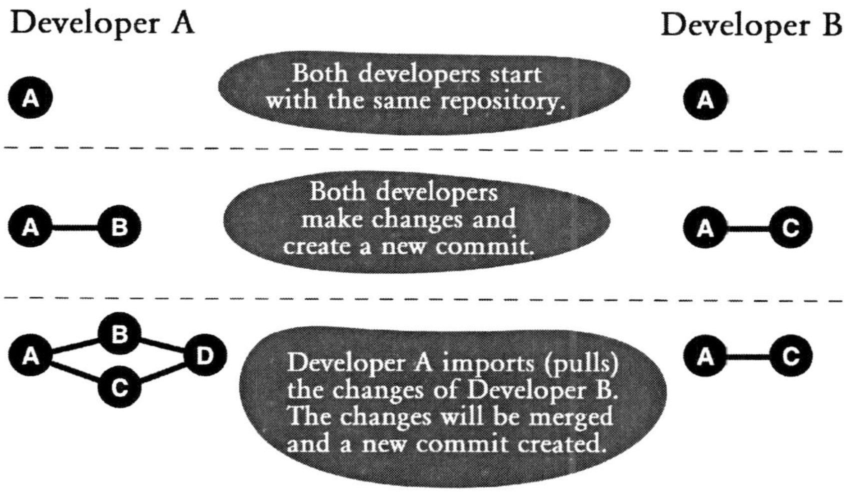

Figure 1.4: Branches are created by developers working in parallel

In the previous example, a branch was created unplanned, simply because two developers were working in parallel on the same software. Of course you can initiate targeted branching in Git and create a branch explicitly (see Figure

1.5). Explicit branching is often done to coordinate a parallel development of features.

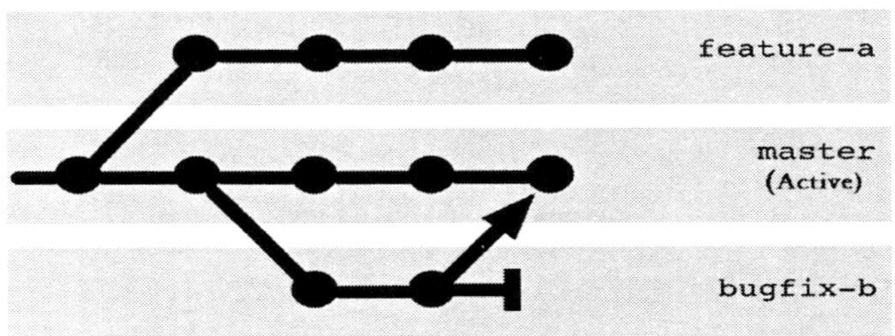

Figure 1.5: Explicit branches for different tasks

Repository pulls and pushes can be explicitly done to determine which branches are transferred. In addition to simple branching and merging, you can also do the following with branches:

- **Transplant a branch:** Commits in a branch can be moved to another repository.
- **Transfer certain changes only:** Individual commits of a branch can be copied to another branch. This is called cherry-picking.
- **Clean up history:** A branch's history can be transformed, sorted and deleted. This would make the history better documentation for the project. This is called interactive rebasing.

Summary

After reading this chapter, you should now be familiar with the basic concepts of Git. Even if you now put the book down (which we hope not!), you can participate in a keynote discussion on distributed version control systems, the necessity and usefulness of hashes as well as permanent branching and merging in Git.

You may be asking yourself the following questions, though.

- What do I use these general concepts to manage my project?
- How do I coordinate the many repositories?
- How many branches do I need?
- How do I integrate my build server?

For the first question, read the next chapter right away. There you will find the specifics of the commands for creating a repository, versioning and replacing commits between repositories. For the other questions, there are chapters with detailed workflows.

If you are a busy executive still trying to decide whether or not to use Git, then take a look at the discussion of the limits of Git in Chapter 26, "Git's Shortcomings."

Chapter 2
Getting Started

You can try out Git right away if you'd like. This chapter describes how to set up your first project. It shows commands for versioning changes, viewing the history and exchanging versions with other developers.

Setting up Git

First you need to install Git. You will find everything you need on the Git website:

http://git-scm.com/download

Git is highly configurable. To start, it is sufficient to submit your user name and e-mail address with the **config** command.

```
> git config --global user.email "hans@mustermann.de"
```

Your First Git Project

It is best if you use a separate project to test Git. Start with a simple small project. Our example shows a tiny project called **first-steps** with two text files.

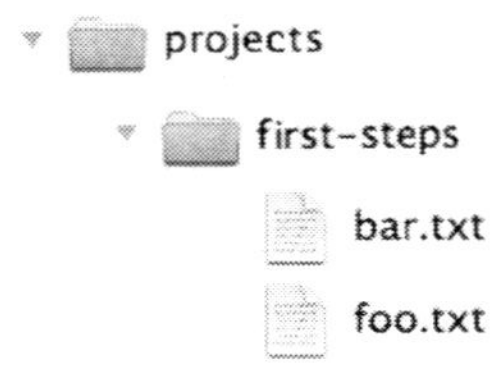

Figure 2.1: Our sample project

Make a copy before you play with the example in your pet project! It is not so easy in Git to permanently delete or break something, and Git usually Git warns you if you are going to do something “dangerous.” Nevertheless, it is better to take precautions.

Creating a repository

First, you need to create a repository in which the history of the project will be stored. You do this by using the **init** command in the project directory. A project directory with a repository is called a workspace.

```
> cd /projects/first-steps
> git init
Initialized empty Git repository in /projects/first-steps/.git/
```

The **init** command above created a repository located in a hidden directory named **.git**. Be warned that the directory may not show in Windows Explorer or Mac Finder.

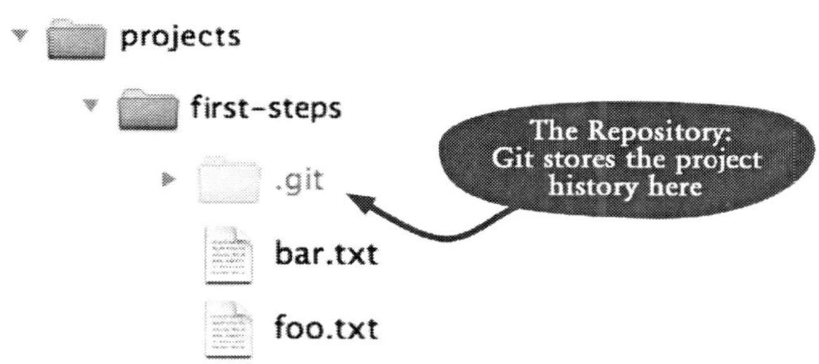

Figure 2.2: The directory where the repository is located

Your First Commit

Next, you are going to add **foo.txt** and **bar.txt** files to the repository. In Git, a project version is called a commit, and is achieved in two steps. First, use the **add** command to determine which files should be included in the next commit. Second, use the **commit** command to transmit the changes to the repository and assign a commit hash that identifies the new commit. Here the hash is 2f43cd0, but yours might be different, depending on the contents of your files.

```
> git add foo.txt bar.txt
```

```
> git commit --message "Sample project imported."
```

```
master (root-commit) 2f43cd0] Sample project imported.
2 files changed, 2 insertions(+), 0 deletions(-)
create mode 100644 bar.txt
create mode 100644 foo.txt
```

Checking the Status

Now change the content of the **foo.txt** file, delete the **bar.txt** file, and add a new file named **bar.html**. The **status** command shows all changes since the last commit.

Note that the new file **bar.html** is shown as untracked, because it has not been registered using the **add** command.

```
> git status

# On branch master
# Changed but not updated:
# (use "git add/rm <file>..." to update what will be committed)
# (use "git checkout -- <file>..." to discard changes in
#                                             working directory)
#
#      deleted:   bar.txt
#      modified:  foo.txt
#
# Untracked files:
# (use "git add <file>..." to include in what will be committed)
#
#      bar.html
no changes added to commit (use "git add" and/or "git commit -a")
```

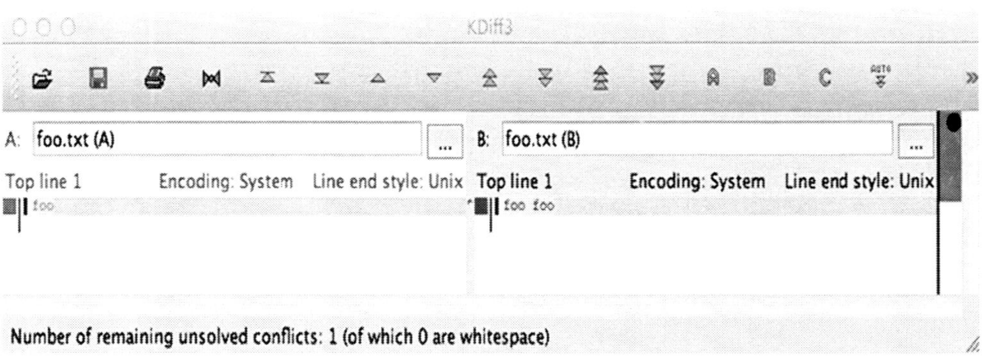

Figure 2.3: Diff representation in graphical tool (kdiff3)

If you want to see more details, use the **diff** command to display each modified row. Many people find the output of **diff** difficult to read. Fortunately, there are a whole range of tools and development environments that can show the changes more clearly (See Figure 2.3).

```
> git diff foo.txt

diff --git a/foo.txt b/foo.txt
index 1910281..090387f 100644
```

```
--- a/foo.txt
+++ b/foo.txt
@@ -1 +1 @@
-foo
\ No newline at end of file
+foo foo
\ No newline at end of file
```

Committing after Changes

All changes must be reported to every new commit. Use the **add** command for modified and new files and use the **rm** command for deleted files.

```
> git add foo.txt bar.html

> git rm bar.txt

rm 'bar.txt'
```

Calling the **status** command again shows what will be included in the next commit.

```
> git status

# On branch master

# Changes to be committed:
#   (use "git reset HEAD <file>..." to unstage)
#
#       new file:   bar.html
#       deleted:    bar.txt
#       modified:   foo.txt
#
```

Use the **commit** command to commit these changes.

```
> git commit --message "Some changes."

[master 7ac0f38] Some changes.

 3 files changed, 2 insertions(+), 2 deletions(-)
 create mode 100644 bar.html
 delete mode 100644 bar.txt
```

Displaying the History

The **log** command displays the project history. All commits are shown in chronologically descending order.

```
> git log

commit 7ac0f38f575a60940ec93c98de11966d784e9e4f
Author: Rene Preissel <rp@eToSquare.de>
Date: Thu Dec 2 09:52:25 2010 +0100

    Some changes.

commit 2f43cd047baadc1b52a8367b7cad2cb63bca05b7
Author: Rene Preissel <rp@eToSquare.de>
Date: Thu Dec 2 09:44:24 2010 +0100

    Sample project imported.
```

Collaboration with Git

You now have a workspace with project files and a repository with a history of the project. In a classic centralized version system, such as CVS and Subversion, each developer has his/her own workspace, but all developers share a common repository. In Git, each developer has his/her own workspace with a separate repository, hence a full-fledged version control system that does not rely on a central server. Developers working together on a project can exchange commits in their repositories. To test this, let's create a new workspace that simulates the activities of a second developer.

Cloning A Repository

The new developer needs his/her own copy (called a clone) of the repository. It contains all the information that includes the original and the entire project history. Run this **clone** command to make a clone.

```
> git clone /projects/first-steps /projects/first-steps-clone
```

```
Cloning into first-steps-clone...
done.
```

The project structure will look like the one in Figure 2.4.

Figure 2.4: The sample project and its clone

Getting Changes from Another Repository

Modify the **first-steps/foo.txt** file and then do the following to create a new commit.

```
> cd /projects/first-steps
```

```
> git add foo.txt
```

```
> git commit --message "A change in the original."
```

The new commit is now stored in the original **first-steps** repository, but is still missing from the clone (**first-steps-clone**) repository. To better understand the situation, we are showing the log for **first-steps**:

```
> git log --oneline
```

```
a662055 A change in the original.
7ac0f38 Some changes.
2f43cd0 Sample project imported.
```

In the next step, modify the **first-steps-clone/bar.html** file in the clone repository and then do the following.

```
> cd /projects/first-steps-clone

> git add bar.html

> git commit --message "A change in the clone."

> git log --oneline

1fcc06a A change in the clone.
7ac0f38 Some changes.
2f43cd0 Sample project imported.
```

You now have a new commit in each of the two repositories. Next, we will transfer the new commit in the original repository to the clone using the **pull** command. When we created the clone repository, the path to the original repository was also stored in the clone, so a **pull** command would know where to pick up new commits.

```
> cd /projects/first-steps-clone

> git pull

remote: Counting objects: 5, done.
remote: Compressing objects: 100% (2/2), done.
remote: Total 3 (delta 0), reused 0 (delta 0)
Unpacking objects: 100% (3/3), done.
From /projects/first-steps
   7ac0f38..a662055 master -> origin/master
Merge made by recursive.
 foo.txt |      2 +-
 1 files changed, 1 insertions(+), 1 deletions(-)
```

The **pull** command has picked up the new changes from the original repository, compared them with local changes in the clone and merged both changes in the workspace and created a new commit it. This is called a *merge*.

Attention! In some cases there will be conflicts when merging. In such an event, Git cannot automatically merge the versions. In this case, you need to manually clean up the files first and then confirm the changes with a commit.

A new **log** command displays the result of the merge after the pull. This time we use a graphical version of the log.

```
> git log --graph

9e7d7b9 Merge branch 'master' of /projects/first-steps

*
|\
| * a662055 A change in the original.
* | 1fcc06a A change in the clone.
|/
* 7ac0f38 Some changes.
* 2f43cd0 Sample project imported.
```

The history is no longer linear. In the graph you can see very clearly the parallel development (the two commits in the middle) and then the merge commit with which the branches were merged again (at the top).

Picking up Changes from Any Repository

Used without a parameter, the **pull** command will only work in a clone repository, since a clone has a link to the original repository. When you do a pull, you can specify the path to any repository so that you can fetch changes in a development branch.

Let's now pull changes in the clone to the original repository.

```
> cd /projects/first-steps

> git pull /projects/first-steps-clone master

remote: Counting objects: 8, done.
remote: Compressing objects: 100% (4/4), done.
remote: Total 5 (delta 0), reused 0 (delta 0)
Unpacking objects: 100% (5/5), done.
From /projects/first-steps-clone
 * branch            master →  FETCH_HEAD
```

```
Updating a662055..9e7d7b9
Fast-forward
 bar.html |    2 +-
 1 files changed, 1 insertions(+), 1 deletions(-)
```

Creating A Repository for Sharing

In addition to the **pull** command that takes commits from another repository, there is also a **push** command that transfers commits to another repository. However, the **push** command should be applied only to a repository where no developer is working. The best way is to create a repository with no workspace in it. Such a repository is called a bare repository. You use the **--bare** option of the **clone** command to create a bare repository. A bare repository can be used as a focal point to which developers transfer their commits (using the **push** command) so that others can pull changes. Figure 2.5 shows a bare repository.

Figure 2.5: A bare repository, a repository with no workspace

```
> git clone --bare /projects/first-steps
                   /projects/first-steps-bare.git

Cloning into bare repository first-steps-bare.git...
done.
```

Uploading Changes with push

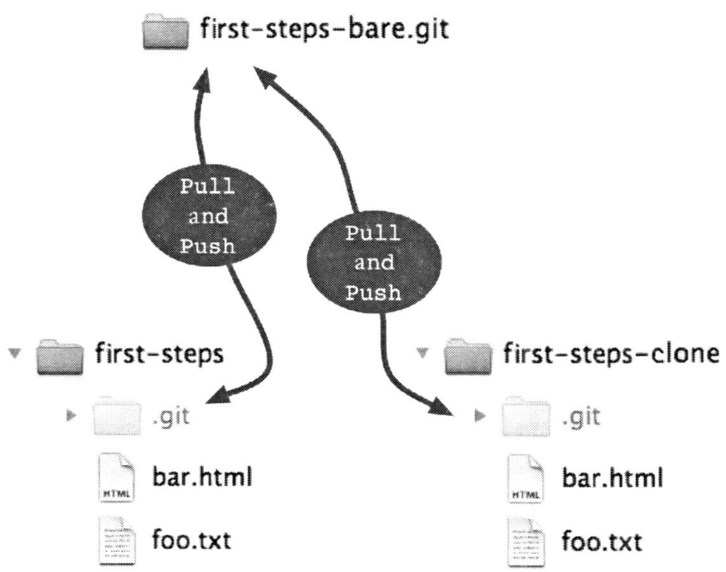

Figure 2.6: Sharing through a shared repository

To demonstrate the **push** command, change the **first-steps/foo.txt** file again and do the following to create a new commit.

```
> cd /projects/first-steps

> git add foo.txt

> git commit --message "More changes in the original."
```

Then transfer this commit using the **push** command to the shared repository (See Figure 2.6). This command expects the same parameters as the **pull** command, the path to the repository and the branch to use.

```
> git push /projects/first-steps-bare.git master

Counting objects: 5, done.
Delta compression using up to 2 threads.
Compressing objects: 100% (2/2), done.
Writing objects: 100% (3/3), 293 bytes, done.
Total 3 (delta 0), reused 0 (delta 0)
Unpacking objects: 100% (3/3), done.
To /projects/first-steps-bare.git/
    9e7d7b9..7e7e589 master -> master
```

Pull: Picking up Changes

To bring the changes to the clone repository, you use the **pull** command with the path to the shared repository.

```
> cd /projects/first-steps-clone

> git pull /projects/first-steps-bare.git master

remote: Counting objects: 5, done.
remote: Compressing objects: 100% (2/2), done.
remote: Total 3 (delta 0), reused 0 (delta 0)
Unpacking objects: 100% (3/3), done.
From ../first-steps-bare
 * branch      master      -> FETCH_HEAD
Updating 9e7d7b9..7e7e589
Fast-forward
 foo.txt |    2 +-
 1 files changed, 1 insertions(+), 1 deletions(-)
```

Attention! If another developer has done a push before us, the **push** command will reject the transfer. Then, the new updates by the other developer must first be picked up with a pull and merged locally.

Summary

- **Workspace and repository:** A workspace is a directory that contains a repository in a **.git** subdirectory. You use the **init** command to create a repository in the current directory.

- **Commit:** A commit defines one version for all the files in the repository and describes when, where and by whom the version was created. Use the **add** command to determine which files to be included in the next commit and then use the **commit** command to create a new commit.
- **Getting information:** The **status** command shows which files have been modified locally and what changes will be incorporated into the next commit. The **log** command shows the commit history. The **diff** command can be used to show the differences between two versions of a file.
- **Clone:** The **clone** command creates a copy of a repository called a clone. In general, every developer has a full clone of the project repository with the entire project history in his/her workspace. With this clone, he/she can work independently without connecting to a server.
- **Push and pull: push** and **pull** are commands for sharing commits between local and remote repositories.

Chapter 3
What Is A Commit?

The most important concept in Git is the commit. Git manages versions of software, and each version is stored as a commit in a repository. A commit always spans the entire project. With a commit, a copy of each file in the project is stored in the repository.

Figure 3.1 shows the summary of important information about a commit that you created using **git log -stat -1**.

```
commit 9acc5d5efec1d2d62f7e98bcc3880cda762cb831
Author: Bjørn Stachmann <bstachmann@yahoo.de>
Date:   Sat Dec 18 18:20:45 2010 +0100

    Section about the commit.

book/commits/commits.tex | 28 +++++++++++++++++++++++++---
1 files changed, 25 insertions(+), 3 deletions(-)
```

Figure 3.1: Information about a commit

The first line is the commit hash 9acc5d5e ... cb831, followed by information about the author, the time the commit was made and a comment. Finally, a summary of what files have changed since the previous version. What the summary does not show: that this commit contains not only the modified file **commits.tex**, but all the files in the project. For each commit Git calculates a 40-character unique code, called the commit hash. If you know this hash, you can restore the files in the project from the repository as they were held at the time of the commit. In Git restoring a version is referred to as *checkout*.

Access Permissions and Timestamps

Git stores access permissions (POSIX File Permissions: Read, Write, Execute) for each file, but not the modification time. At checkout the modification time is set to the current time.

Why isn't the modification timestamp saved? The reason for this is that many build tools use the modification time as the trigger for the re-building of files: If the last change is later than the last build result, make a new build. Since Git always uses the current time as the modification time at checkout, it also makes sure tools will follow the build process correctly.

The add and commit Commands

A commit takes all changes, including newly added files and deleted files. The only exceptions are files in the **.gitignore** file (**.gitignore** is discussed in Chapter 4).

Step by Step
All Changes in One Commit
We can create a commit using the **add** and **commit** commands in two steps.

1.Register changes. Use the **add** command to register changes that will be included in the next commit. The **--all** option indicates all changes will be included.

```
> git add --all
```

2. Create a commit. A new commit will be created.

```
> git commit
```

Revisiting the Commit Hash

At first glance, the 40-character commit hash is a bit long. Other version control systems use simple sequential numbers (as in Subversion) or version names such as 1:17 (as in CVS).

However, there are good reasons why the developers of Git have opted for the hash.

- A commit hash may be generated locally. Communication with other computers or a central server is not required. You can create a new commit anytime, anywhere. The commit hash is calculated from the contents of files and the metadata (author, commit time). The probability that two different changes get the same commit hash is extremely low. After all, there are 2^{160} different values at disposal.
- Even more important is this: the commit hash is more than just a name for a software version. It is also its sum. With the Git **fsck** command you can check the integrity of the repository. If the content does not match the hash, an error like the following will be reported.

```
> git fsck
error: sha1 mismatch 2b6c746e5e20a64032bac627f2729f72a9cba4ee
error: 2b6c746e5e20a64032bac627f2729f72a9cba4ee:
object corrupt or missing
```

You can also specify a shortened commit hash. Mostly just a few characters to identify a commit. If you specify too few characters, Git will display an error message.

```
> git checkout 9acc5d5efec1d2d62f7e98bcc3880cda762cb831
```

```
> git checkout 9acc
```

It is also possible to use a meaningful name (such as **release-1.2.3**) for a commit. This is called a tag.

```
> git checkout release-1.2.3
```

The Commit History

Not only does the repository contain individual commits, it also stores the relationships between the commits. Every time you change the software and confirm this with a commit, Git remembers the previous versions of this commit. A graph of commits can be drawn to show the development of the project (See Figure 3.2).

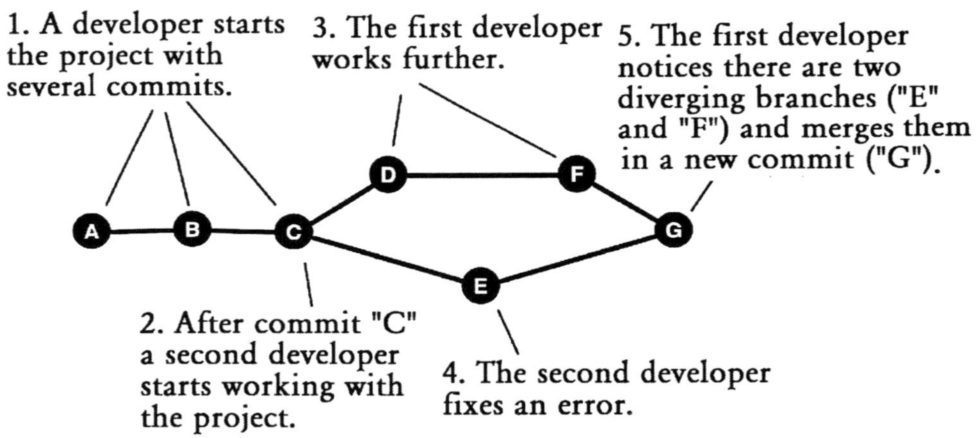

Figure 3.2 : Commit history

It is interesting when multiple developers work simultaneously on a piece of software. Often branches are created in the commit graph, such as in node C, and re-merged, as in G.

A Slightly Different Way of Looking at Commits

You can view a commit as a frozen version level, but it can also be regarded as a set of changes introduced in relation to the previous commit. We also speak of a diff or a change set. So the repository is also a history of changes.

Step by Step
Differences between commits

The **diff** command shows the differences between two commits.

a. Two commits

You can get a complete list of differences between two commits. Instead of using commit hashes, you can also specify symbolic names (branches, tags, HEAD, etc.)

```
> git diff 77d231f HEAD
```

b. Differences from its predecessor

Using ^! with the **diff** command shows the differences from its immediate predecessor.

```
> git diff 77d231f^!
```

c. Limit to file(s)

You can restrict showing only the differences on files or directories.

```
> git diff 77d231f 05bcfd1 - book/bisection/
```

d. Change statistics

Or you can use the **--stat** option to show only the number of changes per file.

```
> git diff --stat 77d231f 05bcfd1
```

Many Different Histories of the Same Project

Initially, the distributed architecture of Git needs some getting used to. In a central version control system (such as CVS or Subversion) there is a central server that contains the history of the project. In Git, however, each developer has his/her own clone of the repository (sometimes more). When a developer creates a commit, this is done locally. His/her repository then will have a different history from the repositories of the other developers, who have cloned the same project.

Each repository can tell its own story. Commits between repositories can be shared using the **fetch**, **pull** and **push** commands. In addition, the **merge** command can make different histories merge again.

In many projects there is a repository (usually on the project server) that contains the official history of the project. Such a repository is called the blessed repository. However, this is just a convention. From a technical perspective, all clones are equal. For example, if the main repository is damaged, another clone can do its job.

A very large project can be distributed across multiple repositories. In this case, there is a main repository, which in turn contains the repositories for the subprojects. Such repositories are called submodules.

Step by Step
Showing the Commit History

The **log** command shows the commit history.

a. Simple log output

```
> git log

commit 2753f19072d332dc550f5ec0612a4486ffe3ab4a
Author: Bjørn Stachmann <bstachmann@yahoo.de>
Date:   Sat Dec 25 11:30:32 2010 +0100

    TODO indented for illustration.

commit e0ffbdbd9f183e405b280a6c3a970bd860d3de81
Author: Bjørn Stachmann <bstachmann@yahoo.de>
...
```

b. Some useful options

```
> git log -n 3       # Only the last three commits
> git log --oneline # Only one line per commit
> git log --stat     # Only show statistics
```

The **log** command may not necessarily show all the commits in the repository. Usually, only the predecessors of the current commits are shown.

The **log** command has several options that allow you to determine which commits are displayed in what format. Some of the more frequently used options are shown below.

Output Limit: -n

It is often useful to limit the output. The following example shows only the last 3 commits:

```
> git log -n 3
```

Formatting Output: --format, --oneline

The format for the log output can be controlled using **--format**. For example, **--format=fuller** provides many details. Here is a quick overview of the **--oneline** option.

```
> git log --oneline
```

```
2753f19 TODO indented for illustration.
e0ffbdb Note.
4200ba2 Section on different histories of the same project.
...
```

Change statistics: --stat, --shortstat

Also useful are the statistics: **--stat** shows which files have been changed. **--dirstat** shows all directories that contain files that have changed, and **--shortstat** shows a short summary of how many files were changed, added and deleted.

```
> git log --shortstat --oneline
```

```
753f19 TODO indented for illustration.
 1 files changed, 2 insertions (+), 2 deletions (-)
e0ffbdb Note.
 1 files changed, 27 insertions (+), 4 deletions (-)
4200ba2 Section on different histories of the same project.
 1 files changed, 15 insertions (+), 6 deletions (-)
...
```

Option: log --graph

You can use the **--graph** option to view the relationships between commits.

```
> git log --graph --oneline
```

```
*   6d7f278 Merge branch 'master' into editorial
|\
| * 419b389 merge: built-in formatting.
| |\
| | * 8f5b053 Quick Start: Formatting installed.
```

```
| | * 5f22c8d New Macros for formatting.
| |/
* | Ab36269 TODOs
* | C2cae84 intro to the first steps.
|/
*   63788eb merge: Section 'Examples and notation' added.
```

Summary

- **Repository:** The project repository resides in the **.git** directory. It contains the history of the project in the form of commits. Because Git is distributed, a project often has many repositories with different histories. Git is designed so that it can merge these histories again if necessary.
- **Commit (also called version, revision, or changeset):** The **commit** command creates a commit. A commit stores a defined state of the project. It includes the state of all the files in the project. Each commit contains metadata about the author and the commit date. In particular, Git stores the predecessor/successor relationship. The relations form a version graph of the project. The **log** command displays the commits from the repository.
- **Commit hash:** A commit hash identifies a commit. At the same time it serves as a checksum to verify the integrity of the stored software object. A commit hash is 40 characters long.

Chapter 4 Multiple Commits

A new commit does not have to accept any changes from the workspace. In fact, Git gives the user full control here. In the extreme case, it can be determined what changes should be incorporated in the next commit.

A commit occurs in two steps. First, all changes are collected in a buffer using the **add** command. This buffer is called the staging area or index. Next, the changes from the staging area are transferred to the repository using the **commit** command.

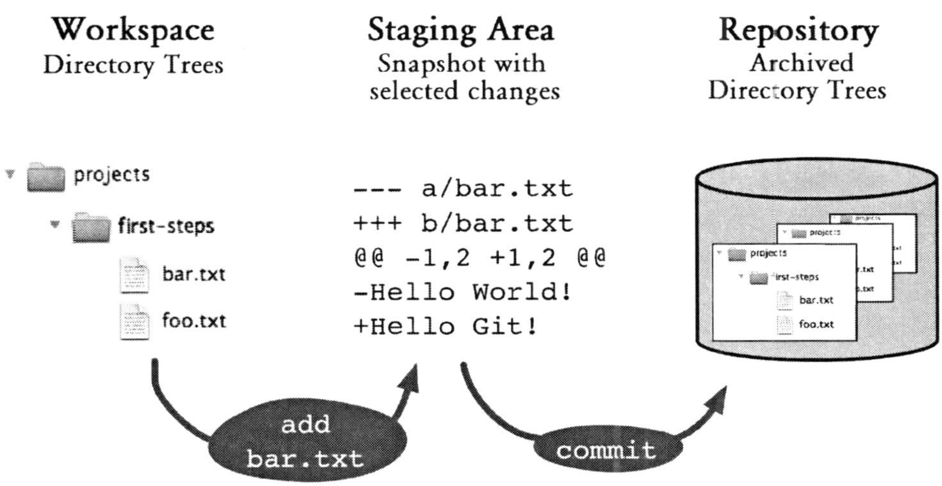

Figure 4.1: The route of changes in the repository

The status Command

The **status** command shows what changes are currently available in the workspace and which of them are already registered in the staging area for the next commit.

```
> git status

# On branch staging
# Changes to be committed:
#    (use "git reset HEAD <file>..." to unstage)
#
# modified: bar.txt
#
# Changed but not updated:
#    (use "git add <file>..." to update what will be committed)
#   (use "git checkout -- <file>..." to discard changes in ...
#
# modified:    foo.txt
#
# Untracked files:
#    (use "git add <file>..." to include in what will be committed)
#
# new.txt
no changes added to commit (use "git add" and/or "git commit -a")
```

The output shows various headings:

- **Changes to be committed:** Lists the files for which changes are to be included in the repository with the next commit.
- **Changed but not updated:** Lists the files that have changed, but have not been registered for the next commit.
- **Untracked files:** Lists all new files.

It helps that Git indicates what command can be used to change the status again. For example, you can use this command to unstage **blah.txt**.

```
git reset HEAD blah.txt
```

CVS and Subversion users may find the use of the term *update* here confusing. In those systems, "update" means the acquisition of changes from the repository into the workspace. In Git, however, update is the incorporation of changes from the workspace into the staging area. This is exactly the opposite direction. Babylon sends its regards.

If there are many changes, you can use the **--short** option to make the output more compact. For instance,

```
> git status --short

M  blah.txt
 M foo.txt
 M bar.txt
?? new-file.txt
```

Step by Step
Selective Commits

A new commit is created. However, it should not include all updates. Here you can select all files or some files only.

1. View the changes

```
> git status
```

Under the headings "Changed but not updated" and "Untracked files" the **status** command shows the files that are not yet registered for the next commit.

2. Collect the changes

Use the **add** command to add the changes to the staging area. You can specify the file paths individually. Or, you can specify a directory to include new and changed files from all subdirectories. The **add** command can be called many times and you can also use wildcards * and ? to specify paths.

```
> git add foo.txt bar.txt # selected files
> git add dir/ # a directory and everything underneath
> git add.  # current directory and everything underneath
```

If you want even finer control, you can use the interactive mode by using the **--interactive** option. Then, you can select individual code fragments and, in extreme cases, individual lines of code to register for the commit.

3. Create a commit
Finally, apply the changes with a commit.

```
> git commit
```

After this the staging area will be empty. The workspace is not affected by the commit. Changes that were not added with **add**, remain in the workspace.

Selective commits can be very useful to separate changes from one another. Example: A new class has been created. Alongside a few mistakes in other classes have been corrected. Separating the changes into several commits makes the history clearer and makes it easier to selectively deliver single bug fixes earlier (cherry-picking).

However, you should keep in mind that selective commits can create in the repository software versions that have never existed locally. They have therefore never been tested and in the worst case may not even compile. We recommend that you avoid selective commits if possible. It is often sufficient to make a note that you want to fix an error, rather than fix it right away.

The Staging Area Stores Snapshots

One thing you should know about the staging area: it is more than just a list of files for the next commit. It stores not only locations of changes, but also what have changed. For this purpose Git generates a snapshot of the affected files with exactly the selected changes. Figure 4.2 illustrates this. In Line 1, the workspace, the staging area and the repository are still the same. Then, the developer working on the file makes some changes in his workspace (Line 2). He then uses the **add** command to transfer the changes to the staging area, but not yet to the repository (Line 3)

In Line 4, the developer changes the file again. Now all the three areas have different contents. A **commit** command transmits the first change to the repository (Line 5). The second change is still in the workspace. The developer then uses the **add** command to transfer it to the staging area (Line 6).

Step by Step
What Is in the Staging Area? What Is Not?

Changes were registered using the **add** command for the next commit. Afterward, further changes were made in the workspace. The **diff** command shows what is going on.

a. What is in the staging area?

Changes that have already been added using the **add** command to the staging area with the **--staged** option will be shown as staged. The following command displays the differences between the staging area and the current HEAD commit in the repository.

```
> git diff --staged # staging vs. repository
```

b. What is not registered yet?

Without any options, the **diff** command shows the local changes in the workspace that are not registered yet, in other words the difference between the staging area and the workspace.

```
> git diff  # staging vs. workspace
```

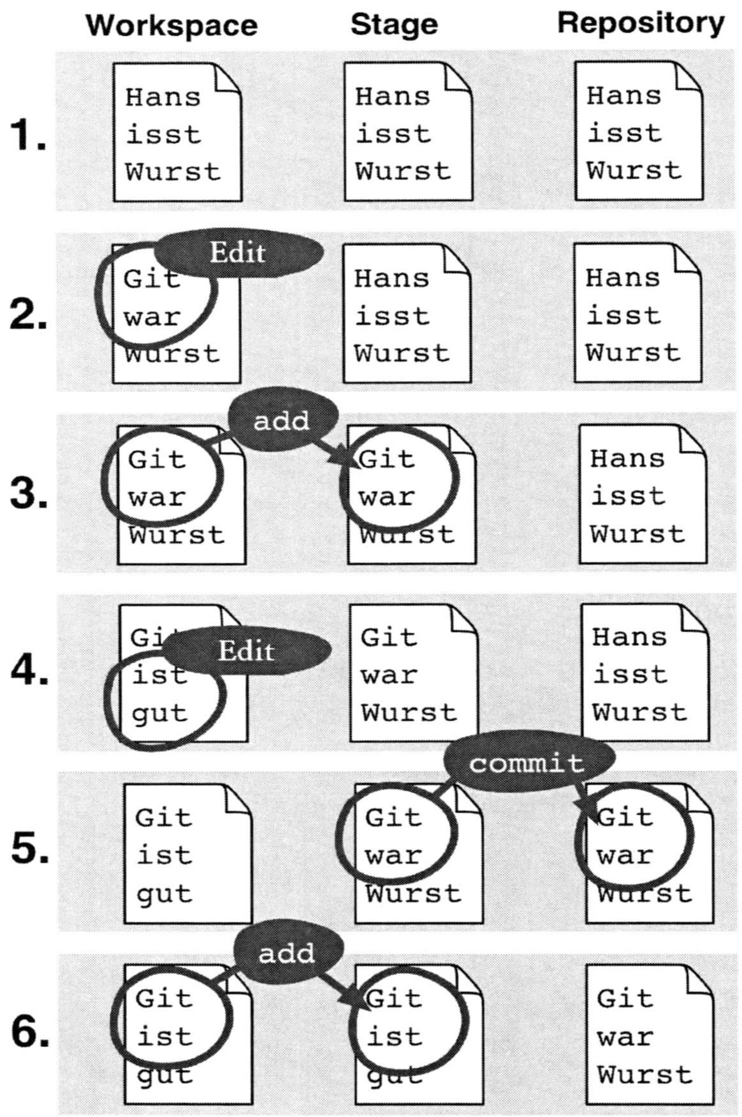

Figure 4.2: Changes from the workspace are copied to the staging area and to the repository

What To Do with Changes That Are Not To Be Committed?

As it happens, there are things that you do not want to commit, including:

- experimental changes for debugging purposes
- changes that are added by accident
- changes that are not ready yet
- changes in generated files

Git offers several ways to deal with them:

- Reset experimental changes or changes made by accident using the **reset** command
- Ignore files that you do not want to commit using **.gitignore**
- Save changes that you might want to commit later with the **stash** command

Step by StepUndoing changes from the Staging Area

The **reset** command resets the staging area. The first parameter HEAD indicates that it is to be reset to the current HEAD version. The second parameter specifies which files or directories are to be reset.

```
> git reset HEAD .
```

or

```
> git reset HEAD foo.txt src/test/
```

The staging area is overwritten during reset. Usually this is not a problem, because the same changes are likely still in the workspace (see Figure 4.2). If the same files were further processed after the **add** command, information may be lost.

Leaving out Unversioned Files with .gitignore

In general, generated files, temporary files created by editors or backups are files you do not want to put under version control. By adding entries in a **.gitignore** file in the root directory of the project you can make these files "invisible" to Git. You can specify file paths and directories in it. The wildcard characters "*" and "&" can also be used. You should know the following about paths: A simple path like **generated/** will make directories that contain the name, such as **src/demo/generated**, ignored everywhere, If the path is prefixed with a /, such as in **/generated/**, then only the exact path—relative to the project's root directory —will be ignored.

```
#
# Simple file path
#
somehow/simultaneous.txt
#
# Directories ending with a "/"
#
generated/
#
# File types as glob expressions
#
*.bak
#
# "!" marked exceptions. "demo.bak"
# will be versioned, but "*.bak"'
# will be excluded.
#
!demo.bak
```

You can create a **.gitignore** file in a subdirectory of your project. In this case, it will affect all files and paths below that directory. This may be useful, for example, if your project is comprised of various programming languages, each of which needs a different configuration.

Note that entries in **.gitignore** only affect files that are not yet managed by Git. If a file is already versioned, the **status** command will display all changes to it, and these can also be registered with the **add** command for the next commit. If you want to ignore files that are already versioned, you can do this with the **--assume-unchanged** option of the **update-index** command.

Stashing

If you are in the middle of something and, say, a fix needs to be written quickly, you often want to start making changes but not commit what you have been doing. In this case the **stash** command can help save changes locally and those changes can be referred to again later.

Step by Step
Saving Changes

The **stash** command saves changes in the workspace and the staging area in a buffer called the stash stack.

```
> git stash
```

Step by Step

Getting Back to Stashed ChangesStashed changes can be retrieved from the stack to the workspace using the **stash pop** command.

a. Retrieve the top-most stashed change

```
> git stash pop
```

b.1. What Is in the Stash Stack?

First, check to see what changes have been stashed.

```
> git stash list

stash@{0}: WIP on master: 297432e Mindmap updated.
stash@{1}: WIP on omaster: 213e335 Introduction to workflow
```

b.2. Retrieve Older Stashed Changes
First, check to see what changes have been stashed.

```
> git stash pop stash@{1}
```

Summary

- **Staging area:** The staging area (also called index) is where you prepare for the next commit. It contains a snapshot of file contents.
- **Adding generated snapshots:** You use the **add** command to create a snapshot of modified files in the staging area. If you change the same files again, the new changes are not automatically included in the next commit.
- **Selective commit:** When you use the **add** command, you can specify which files are to be included in the snapshot. All other files remain unchanged.
- **Selecting sections of code:** With **--interactive** you can even select individual sections of changed rows (hunks). Only these changes are then transmitted as a snapshot in the staging area.
- **Status:** The **status** command shows which files go into the next commit and which files have been modified locally, but are not yet registered in the staging area.
- **Reset the staging area:** With **git reset HEAD .** all files will be reset to the current HEAD version.
- **.gitignore:** In this file, you list files and directories that Git should not manage.
- **Stashing:** With the **stash** command you can stash the current changes in the workspace and the staging area. Later, you can retrieve it again with **git stash pop**.

Chapter 5
The Repository

You can use Git quite well without knowing how the repository works. However, you will have a better understanding of the workflow if you know how Git stores and organizes its data. If you really hate theory, you can skim through this chapter and just read the Step by Step sections.

Git is constructed in two planes. On the upper level you have commands such as **log**, **reset** or **commit**, which are easy to use and offer numerous options and call options. Git developers call these commands porcelain commands.

The layer below it is called plumbing. Here there are a number of simple commands with few options on which to build the porcelain commands. Plumbing commands are rarely used directly. This chapter provides a little insight into the plumbing level of the system.

A Simple and Efficient Storage System

The core of Git is an object database. Here you can store text or binary data, such as the content of a file. You can use the **hash-object** command with the **-w** option (**w** stands for write) to insert a record into the object database.

```
> git hash-object -w hello.txt

28cf67640e502fe8e879a863bd1bbcd4366689e8
```

When you store an object, Git returns a 40-character code. This is the key for the stored object. Keep in mind that you can access the object again later with the key using the **cat-file** command with the **-p** option (**p** stands for print).

```
> git cat-file -p 28cf67640e
Hello World!
```

The implementation of the object database is very efficient. Even in a large project with a very long commit history (such as the Linux kernel, which has more than 200,000 commits and almost two million objects), accessing objects from the repository is almost instantaneous. Git is extremely well suited for projects with a large number of small source files. The boundaries become apparent only when the total data volume of the data gets very large. Those wanting to manage large binary files with a Git repository will not be well served.

Storing Directories: Blob & Tree

To store files and directories Git uses a simple tree with two types of nodes. File contents are unchanged, stored byte by byte as blob objects in the object database. Directories are represented by tree objects that look like this:

```
> git cat-file -p 2790ef78

100644 blob 507d3a30ae9ed53bcf953744c5f5c9391a263356 README
040000 tree 91c7822ab43800b0e3c13049519587df4fd74591 src
```

The tree object contains files and subdirectories, as shown in Figure 5.2. Each entry comes with information about access rights (eg 100644), type (blob or tree), and a hash of the file content and the name of the file or directory.

```
sample-workspace/
    README
    /src
        Hello.java
        World.java
```

Figure 5-1: A small project

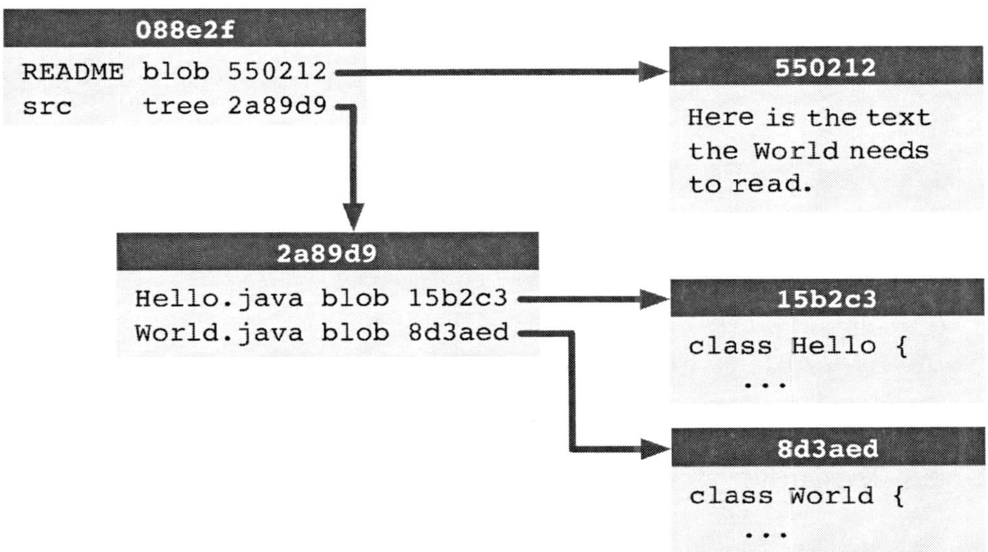

Figure 5.2: Representation of directories in the repository

Identical Data Is Stored Only Once

To save memory, identical data is stored only once. In the following example, the file contents from **foo.txt** and **copy-of-foo.txt** return the same hash, because they are identical:

```
> git hash-object -w foo.txt

a42a0aba404c211e8fdf33d4edde67bb474368a7


> git hash-object -w copy-of-foo.txt
```

```
a42a0aba404c211e8fdf33d4edde67bb474368a7
```

By using this approach, not only does Git save memory, it also gains performance. Many Git operations are fast because they only compare hashes in their algorithms without looking at the actual data.

Compressing Similar Content

Git can do more than just merge identical file content. When programmers are constantly creating new files that differ from their predecessors in only a few lines, Git can save these files using a delta method, which stores only the changes after the original version in pack files.

To do this, use the **gc** command when you want to save space. Git removes any unwanted commits that are no longer accessible from any branch head, and stores the remaining commits in pack files. For projects that contain mostly source code, an amazingly high compression is achieved. Often the size of the unzipped workspace contents with the current version of the project is greater than the size of the Git repository with years of project history.

Is It Bad When Various Files Happen to Get the Same Hash?

That would be bad, because Git identifies content by its hash. Git could therefore provide incorrect data when the contents of various files happen to have the same hash. This is known as a hash collision.

The good news is that a hash collision is an extremely unlikely event. The reason is that there are at least 2^{160}

possible hashes. For instance, after five years the Linux kernel project "only" has about 2^{21} objects in its repository.

In theory, the SHA1 hash algorithm has weaknesses, in which you could find an SHA1 collision with 2^{51} operations. However, a research project at Graz University of Technology tried from 2007 to 2009 to find one (!) such hash collision, and was terminated without success. In summary it is safe to say that security in the context of version control is okay today.

Commits

Commits are stored in the object database. The format is simple:

```
> git cat-file -p 64b98df0

tree 319c67d41a0b3f7464550b41db4bb1584939ad2a
parent 6c7f1ba0828a5b595026e08d2476808105a6b815
author Bjørn Stachmann <bs@test123.de> 1295906997 +0100
committer Bjørn Stachmann <bs@test123.de> 1295906997 +0100

Section on trees & blobs.
```

In addition to metadata, such as the author, committer, date and comment, a commit object contains hashes for other objects in the object database. The tree object describes the contents of the commit. It refers to the project's root directory and, as described above, is represented by trees and blobs. The parent object represents the previous commit.

Object Reuse in the Commit History

Except for the very first commit, every commit has at least one predecessor commit (parent object). Often a commit only changes a few files in a project, and most of the files and directories remain unchanged. Whenever possible Git reuses objects from the previous commit.

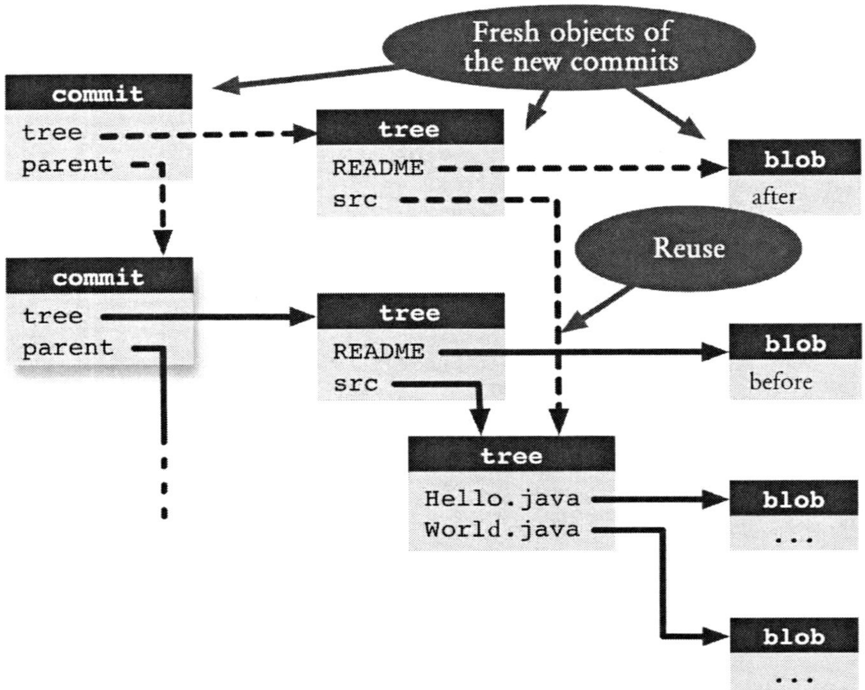

Figure 5.3: Reusing of an object tree

Figure 5.3 shows an example. A commit (represented by the second rectangular with the header "commit" on the second row from the top, with solid arrows) includes a **README** file and a **src** directory containing other files. When a new commit is created (the rectangular with the header "commit" on the first row, with dashed arrows), in which only the **README** file has changed. A new blob object is created for **README**. However, for the **src** directory, the existing tree object and associated blob can still be used.

Renaming, Moving and Copying

In many version control systems you can trace the history of file renames and time changes. Most often this is achieved by using a special command to move or rename files. In Subversion, for example, you move a file with **svn move**. However, Subversion is clueless when the user moves a file by dragging and dropping the file to a new location. In this case, Subversion knows nothing about the move and instead records a file deletion and creates a new file.

Git takes a different approach: it stores no information about which files have been moved. Instead, it employs a rename detection algorithm: If a file is missing from a commit but was still present in the predecessor, Git checks if a file with the same name or very similar content emerges in another location. If this is so, Git assumes that the file has been moved. Figure 5.4 shows this: The **foo.txt** file that has been moved is missing in the second commit. Git then examines all recently added files for one that has similar content and locates it in **src/foo-moved.txt**. This is interpreted as renaming.

```
sample-workspace/          sample-workspace
    foo.txt                     (foo.txt missing)
    /src                         /src
        bar.txt                      bar.txt
                                     foo-moved.txt


(Commit 1)                  (Commit 2)
```

Figure 5.4: A file is moved

Step by Step
Following renames and moving

Git will show which files have been renamed or moved.

1. Get a summary
You activate rename detection using the **log** command with the **-M** option (for "Move"). To format the output, use the **--summary** option to display information about file changes. The problem is, the output is very long. If you like a shorter one, you can filter the output using the **grep** command. The percentage in each line indicates how similar the source and target files are.

```
> git log --summary -M90% | grep -e "^ rename"

rename foo.txt => foo-renamed.txt (90%)
rename src/{before => after}/bar.txt (100%)
```

2. Track the history of a file that has been moved
Use the **log** command with the **--follow** option to continue listing the history of a file beyond renames (works only for a single file). Without this option, the log would end at file renames.

```
> git log --follow foo-renamed.txt
```

Step by Step
Tracking down copies

You can also track data that has been copied using the **-C** option.

```
> git log --summary -C90% | grep -e "^ copy"
```

If necessary, you can use the **--find-copies-harder** option to make Git do the calculation longer. If this option is present, Git will examine all files in a commit, not only those that have been changed.

You can also configure Git so that rename detection is enabled by default. Then, you do not need to specify the **-M** and **--follow** options for each **log** command you issue.

```
> git config diff.renames true
```

Step by Step

Determining the origin of a code section

You want to find out who last changed some lines of code and when.

1. Print the origin information line by line

Git can even determine the origin of lines of code when larger sections of the code were copied or moved from other files. The **blame** command also displays when and by whom a line of code was last modified.

```
> git blame -M -C -C -C copied-together.txt

f5fdbad0 foo.txt  (Rene  2010-11-14 18:30:42 +0100   1) One,
a5b80903 bar.txt  (Bjørn 2011-01-31 21:32:49 +0100   2) Two or
f5fdbad0 foo.txt  (Rene  2010-11-14 18:30:42 +0100   3) Three
```

The **-M** option (M for Move) reveals the copies and moves of a file. The **-C** option also detect copies of files in the same commit. You can also use multiple **-C** options to search for files in other commits. For large repositories this can sometimes take a little longer.

Summary

- **Object database:** The files, directories, and metadata for all commits are stored in this database.
- **SHA1 hash:** You can retrieve objects from the object database using an SHA1 hash. A SHA1 hash is a cryptographic checksum of file contents.

- **Identical data is stored only once:** Objects with the same content have the same SHA1 hash and are stored only once.
- **Similar data is compressed:** For similar data there is a delta method that stores only the changes.
- **Blob:** The content of a file is stored in a blob.
- **Tree:** A directory is stored in an object tree. An object tree contains a list of file names with the SHA1 hash of the content belonging to a blob or a tree.
- **Commit graph:** Commit objects form a commit graph, along with the tree and blob objects.
- **Rename detection:** File rename and move do not have to be reported before a commit. Git recognizes this later by examining the similarities of the file contents. Example: **git log --follow**
- **Who was it:** You can use the **blame** command to determine the origin of lines of code, even if they have been moved or copied.

Chapter 6 Branches

There are two important reasons why version histories do not always run linear, commit by commit:

- Two or more developers worked in parallel on a project.
- Bug fixes for older versions must be created and delivered.

In both cases, branches are created in the commit history graph.

Parallel Development

When more than one developer works on the same piece of software with Git, branches are created in the commit graph. The upper half of Figure 6.1 shows how two independent developers have created succeeding versions (commits **C** and **D**) to commit **B** in their local repositories. Below it you see the repository after a merge (see Chapter 9 on how to do this). It has created a branch. This type of branching can hardly be avoided in parallel development.

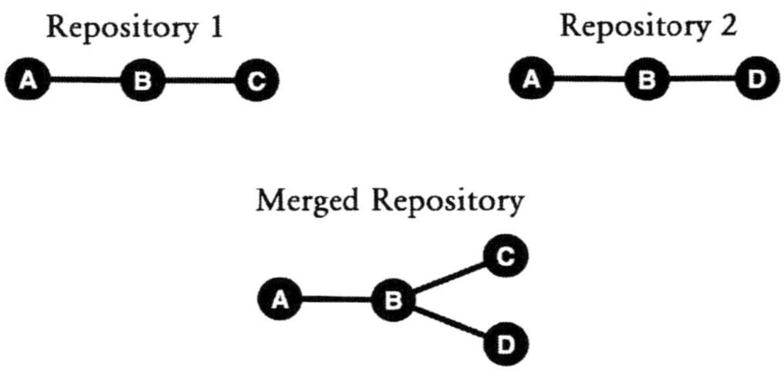

Figure 6.1: Parallel development

Bug Fixes in An Older Version

A branch may get created due to parallel development. In addition, a branch may also get created when fixing bugs in an older software version. Figure 6.2 shows an example: While the developers are working intensively on the version for the upcoming release (commits **C** and **D**), an error in the current software version (commit **B**) is detected. Since the new features in commits **C** and **D** are not ready yet for delivery, a bug fix **E** is created based on commit **B**.

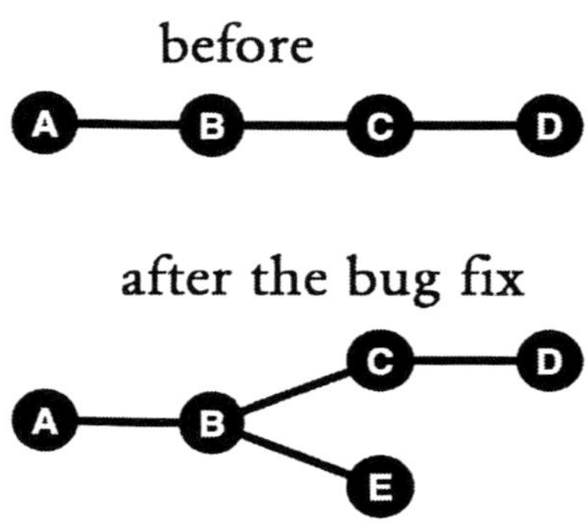

Figure 6.2: Bug fixes in an older version

Branches

In the example in Figure 6.3 you can see on the one hand a **release1** branch for the current release version and the **master** branch for current development. With each new commit, an active branch wanders. The right panel shows how the **release1** branch wanders further with the bug fix.

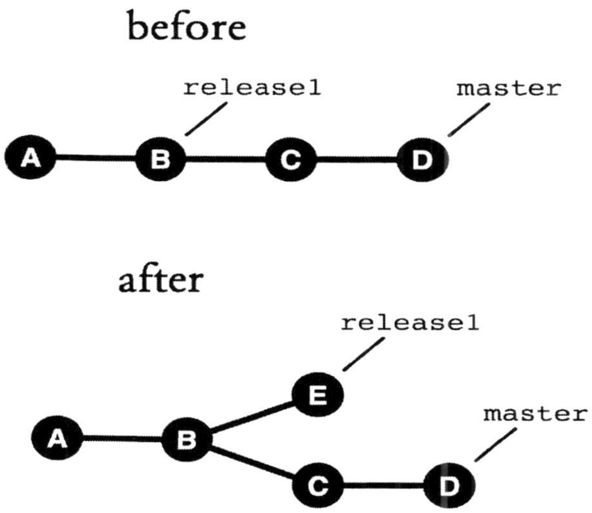

Figure 6.3: Branches in the version graph

Swim Lanes

Branches can be thought of as parallel lines of development. You can visualize this as swim lanes in the commit graph (See Figure 6.4).

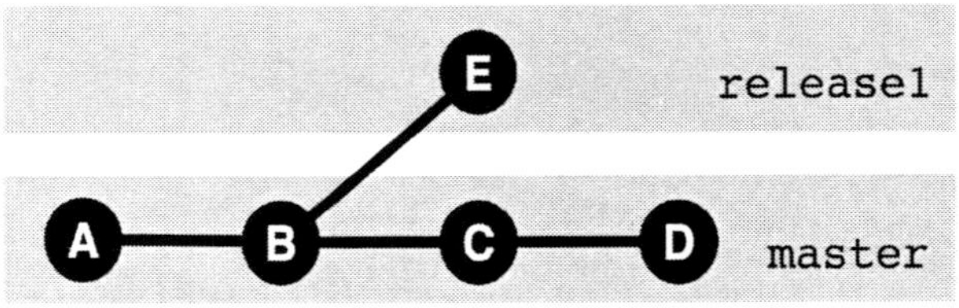

Figure 6.4: Branches as parallel lines of development

Note: Git does not know if a commit is assigned to a branch; the division into lanes is an interpretation that to some extent is arbitrary.

The Active Branch

In a Git repository there is always exactly one active branch. The **branch command** (without options) shows a list of all branches. The active branch is highlighted with an asterisk (*).

```
> git branch

  a-branch
* master
  still-a-branch
```

The active branch will always continue with any new commit, pointing to the most recent commit. You can use the **checkout command** to change the active branch.

```
> git checkout a-branch
```

Step by Step
Creating a branch

A new branch will be created.

1a. Branching off the current commit

```
> git branch a-branch
```

1b. Branching off any arbitrary commit

You can also branch off any arbitrary commit. To do this, you must specify the start commit for the new branch.

```
> git branch still-a-branch 38b7da45e
```

1c. Branching from an existing branch

```
> git branch still-a-branch older-branch
```

2. Switching to the new branch

The **branch** command only creates a new branch, but does not switch you to the new branch. To switch to the new branch, use the **checkout** command.

```
> git checkout a-branch
```

Shortcut: Creating a branch and switch to it

```
> git checkout -b a-branch
```

Step by Step
Checkout denied. What now?

Normally you can use the **checkout** command to bounce back and forth between branches. However, if there are changes in the workspace, you have to decide how to get around these local changes.

1. Checkout

Here is how a checkout may be denied.

```
> git checkout a-branch

error: Your local changes to the following files would be
overwritten by checkout: foo.txt
Please, commit your changes or stash them before you can
```

```
switch branches.
Aborting
```

There are changes in the workspace or the staging area, which were still not confirmed with a commit. You have to decide what to do with the changes.

2a. Commit and switch

```
> git commit --all
> git checkout a-branch
```

2b. Discard the changes and switch
You can force a switch with the **--force** option. However, all local changes will be overwritten!

```
> git checkout --force a-branch
```

2c. Stash and switch
You can stash the changes using the **stash** command (See the section "Stashing" in Chapter 4) and then switch. Later you can retrieve them with the **stash pop** command.

```
> git stash
> git checkout a-branch
```

Resetting A Branch Pointer

The branch pointer to the active branch moves farther with each commit. Therefore, it is rarely necessary to set the branch pointer directly. However, sometimes you lose track of what is happening and would like to return to a previous state. In this case, you can reset the branch pointer with the **reset** command.

```
> git reset --hard 39ea21a
```

Here the pointer is set to the active branch of commit **39ea21a**. The **--hard** option ensures that the workspace and staging area are also set to the state of commit **39ea21a**.

Be warned that **reset --hard** overwrites any changes in the workspace and staging area. You should stash the changes with **git stash** before resetting.

Deleting A Branch

Step by Step
Deleting a branch

You can delete a branch with **branch -d**.

a. Deleting a terminated branch

```
> git branch -d b-branch
```

b. Deleting an open branch

If the branch you are trying to delete is not yet transferred to a different branch, such as the master, Git will give you a warning and refuse to delete it. If you want to delete the branch anyway, use the **-D** option.

```
error: The branch 'b-branch' is not fully merged.
If you are sure you want to delete it, run 'git branch -D b-branch'.

> git brach -D b-branch
Deleted branch b-branch (was 742dcf6).
```

Step by StepRestoring a deleted branch

Git manages branches so that when you delete a branch, Git only deletes the pointer to the commit. The commit objects are still in the repository. You can restore a deleted branch if you know the commit hash in the message you get after deleting a branch.

a. Restoring a branch (commit hash known)

```
> git branch a-branch 742dcf6
```

b.1. Determining the commit hash

If you do not know the commit hash of the branch you want to restore, you can find it using the **reflog** command.

```
> git reflog

d765a1e HEAD@{0}: checkout: moving from b-branch to master
88117f6 HEAD@{1}: merge b-branch: Fast-forward
9332b08 HEAD@{2}: checkout: moving from a-branch to b-branch
441cdef HEAD@{3}: commit: Expanded important stuff
```

b.2. Restoring the branch (with hash from reflog)

```
> git branch b-branch HEAD@{1}
```

Getting Rid of the Commit Objects

The **gc** command (gc for garbage collect) cleans up the repository and removes commit objects that are not reachable from the current branches. If you really want to make sure your repository is clean, then clone it and delete the original.

Summary

- **Branching in the commit graph:** Caused by parallel development and fixing bugs in an older version.
- **Branches:** A branch is a name for a branching in the commit graph. The branch has a pointer to the latest commit in that branching.
- **Active branch:** You normally work off an active branch. When you make a new commit here, the pointer is set to the new commit.
- **Creating a branch:** Use the **branch** command to create a new branch.
- **Checkout:** Use the **checkout** command to switch to another branch.
- **Reflog:** Git records all changes to branch pointers in every commit. This is useful if you want to restore branches you delete by accident.
- **Garbage:** Commits that are not predecessors of any branch should be regarded as garbage. They can be cleaned up with the **gc** command.

Chapter 7 Merging Branches

One of the most important Git operations is the merging of branches with the **merge** command. The underlying algorithms are complex, but the call is easy. You do that by specifying the name of the branch whose changes are to be integrated. Git then creates a new commit that contains the merged content.

Figure 7.1 shows an example: While some developers keep on working on a branch named **feature**, another developer has just fixed an error on the **master** branch (commit **E**). Shortly thereafter, the feature is completed and will also be delivered. The next version on the **master** branch should contain both the fix and the new feature. With the **merge command** carried along the branches, the result is a merge commit (in this case **F**) which has two predecessors (**D** and **E**).

```
> # on the branch "master"

> git merge feature
```

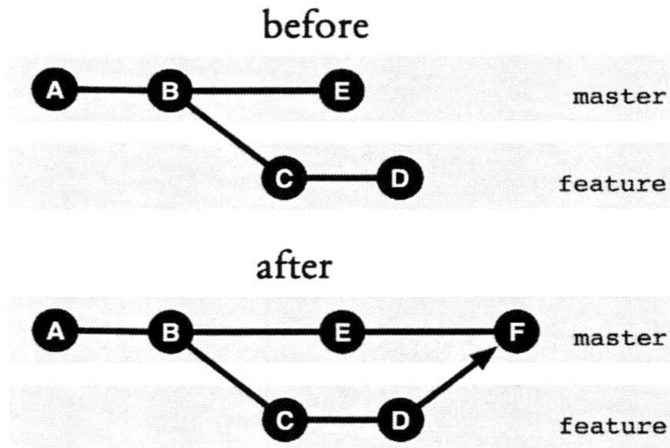

Figure 7.1: Merging branches

What Happens during A Merge?

One of the objectives of Git is to make collaboration of distributed developers as easy as possible. Therefore, to a large extent the **merge** command merges branches automatically, without user interaction. But how is it possible?

Figure 7.2 shows two different versions of a file, in branch **a** and branch **b**, respectively. It is pretty easy to see which rows are different. But which variant is the right one? "Freitag" or "Montag"? "Git" or "Fit"? How should the merge algorithm decide?

The key often lies in the commit history. The trick is to find the last common ancestor. In somewhat simplified terms this is the point where the paths of the branches have separated. If you compare the original version with the variations in the branches, the picture will become clearer.

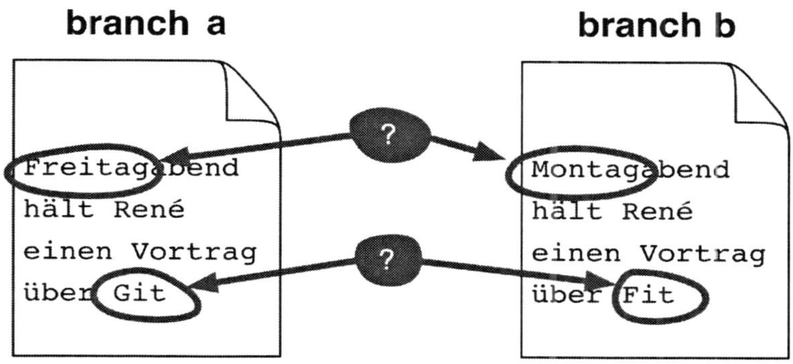

Figure 7.2: Two versions: Which one is correct?

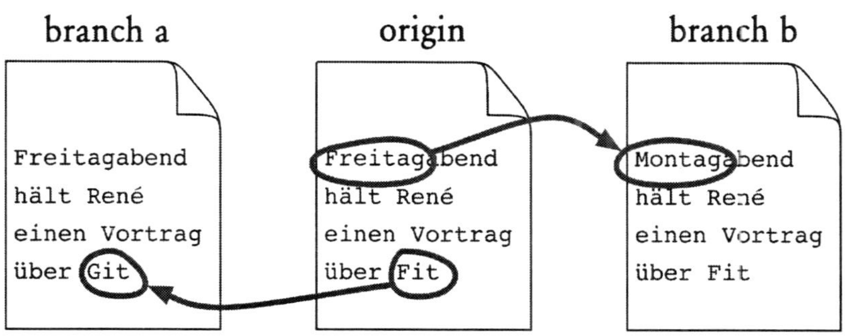

Figure 7.3: 3-way view

In the example in Figure 7.3 you can see that in the first line "Freitagabend" was replaced by "Montagabend" in branch **b**. In branch **a**, the first line was not changed. This is a strong indication that you should take "Montagabend" when merging the two branches. In the same way, it is safe to conclude that you should take "Git" and not "Fit" in the last line. Figure 7.4 shows the result.

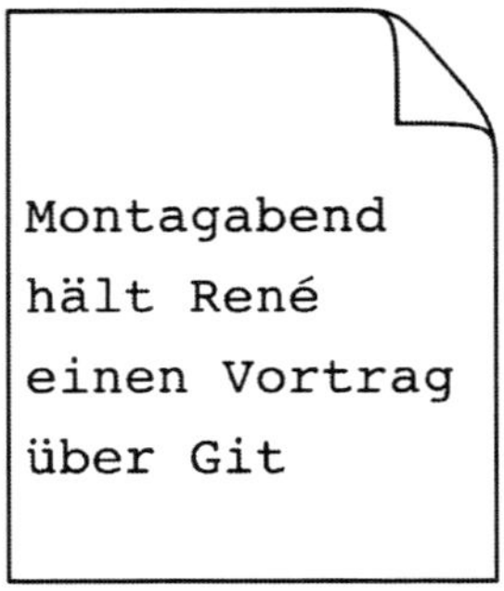

Figure 7.4: Merge result

Indeed, it is not so easy to find the common ancestor. As such, Git implements three different merge algorithms. The default is the recursive algorithm. The classic 3-way and the "octopus" algorithms are also implemented. "Octopus" can bring together many branches simultaneously.

Conflicts

Git is very good at merging changes in program source code when several developers have made changes in multiple places in the software. This often works even if the affected files have been moved or renamed. Unfortunately, there are still always conflicts that Git cannot resolve automatically.**Edit conflicts** occur when two developers have changed the same lines of code differently and Git cannot decide which of the two is the correct change.**Content conflicts** occur when two developers have changed several parts of the code. This happens, for example, when a developer changed a function and another developer changed the same function at the same time.

Edit Conflicts

If Git is unable to resolve a conflict, it will display an error message.

```
> git merge one-branch

Auto-merging foo.txt
CONFLICT (content): Merge conflict in foo.txt
Automatic merge failed; fix conflicts and then commit the result.
```

The following is what happens:

1. Git has not created a commit. Normally Git creates a commit automatically after a merge. In the event of a conflict, you must first resolve the problem and then create a commit manually.
2. In **.git/MERGE_HEAD** there is the commit hash of another branch.
3. The files in the workspace reflect the merge result.
4. Conflict-free merged changes are logged in the staging area, ready for the next commit.
5. Conflict markers are inserted.
6. The points of conflict are not yet registered for the next commit.

The **status** command now displays the files that were automatically merged in the section "Changes to be committed". In the section "Unmerged paths" it shows the files that the user must manually edit.

```
> git status

# On branch master
# You have unmerged paths.
#   (fix conflicts and run "git commit")
#
# Changes to be committed:
#
# modified:   blah.txt
#
```

```
# Unmerged paths:
#   (use "git add <file>..." to mark resolution)
#
# both modified:       foo.txt
#
```

Conflict Markers

A conflict marker shows both variants. First come the lines as they looked on the current branch (HEAD). Next to it you can see how they look like on the other branch (MERGE_HEAD, here **one-branch**):

```
In the early morning dew
<<<<<<< HEAD
to the valley
=======
 for swimming
>>>>>>> one-branch
We're going. Fallera!;
```

For historical reasons, the common ancestor is not displayed by default. However, you can configure the 3-way format:

```
> git config merge.conflictstyle diff3
```

An edit conflict will then be represented as follows:

```
In the early morning dew
<<<<<<< HEAD
to the valley
||||||| merged common ancestors
to mountains
=======
for swimming
>>>>>>> one-branch
We're going Fallera!;
```

Resolving Edit Conflicts

Your best bet to resolve edit conflicts would be to use a merge tool, like kdiff3. You start the merge tool using the **mergetool** command.

```
> git mergetool
```

Here you can resolve the conflicts, save the changes and terminate the application. Afterward, the merged changes will be in the staging area and can be confirmed with a commit.

For binary files, there is no textual conflict marker. Here you have to look at the original versions. Three versions of the file play a role in the conflict: the version on the current branch (ours), the version on the other branch (theirs), and the last common ancestor of these two branches (ancestor). The **show** command can be used to retrieve these versions.

```
> git show :1:picture.png  >ancestor.png
 > git show :2:picture.png  >ours.png
> git show :3:picture.png  >theirs.txt
```

Merge and diff tools usually also show changes in the whitespace. If, for example, a developer has replaced tabs with spaces, all rows will be marked, although the content has probably not changed. The tools usually come with an option to ignore whitespace changes. You should use this option.

It is even better of course if all developers use the same automatic source code formatter, which would then rule out formatting as a source of conflict.

> **Step by StepManual merge**
>
> **1a. Edit the affected files**
> For each conflict point you consider what option you want to take, and then remove the rest of the conflict markers in a text editor. However, you cannot do this with binary files, and only Step 1b is possible.
>
> **1b. Take --ours or --theirs**
> Alternatively, you can also use the **checkout** command to take only their (or others') version of the files completely.
>
> ```
> > git checkout --theirs tests/
> ```
>
> **2. Register the changes**
>
> ```
> > git add .
> ```
>
> **3. Commit**
>
> ```
> > git commit
> ```

Accidents happen! If you make a merge mistake or when trying to revolve a conflict, then you should not continue. Instead, you should explicitly cancel the merge so that there is no trace of merging in the workspace, and so that Git will not mark the next commit a merge commit.

A merge can be canceled using the **reset** command:

```
> git reset --merge
```

What about the Content Conflict?

The real problem is the content conflict, because Git does not recognize it and certainly cannot resolve it automatically. The real danger is when the **merge** command produces a valid merge commit when there is a content conflict.

Attention! Even if all merged versions are correct and Git has reported no editing conflicts, a merge commit may be broken!

If you want to prevent content conflicts from messing with software versions, you should do more:

- **Protection through automated tests:** If these are carried out regularly and you have a good coverage, you will discover contents conflicts quickly.
- **Assertions, pre- and post-conditions:** The more assertions you check explicitly, the sooner you will recognize problems.
- **Clear interfaces, loose coupling:** The cleaner the architecture is at this point, the less likely surprising side effects of code changes in different places will creep in.
- **Static type checking:** If your programming language supports this, problems caused by signature changes will be detected at compile time.

Incidentally, it is valid to specify multiple branches to be merged in the **merge** command. This is what we call an octopus merge.

Fast-Forward Merges

Often the following occurs: There are several branches, but work continues only on one branch. In the project in Figure 7.5, the developers have been developing on **a-branch**, and nothing is happening on **b-branch**. When executing a merge with **a-branch** on **b-branch**, Git makes it simple: It simply moves the pointer forward. There will be no merge commit. This is called a fast-forward merge.

```
> git checkout b-branch

> git merge a-branch
```

```
Updating 9d4caed..9332b08
Fast-forward
 foo.txt    |    2 +-
1 files changed, 1 insertions(+), 1 deletions(-)
```

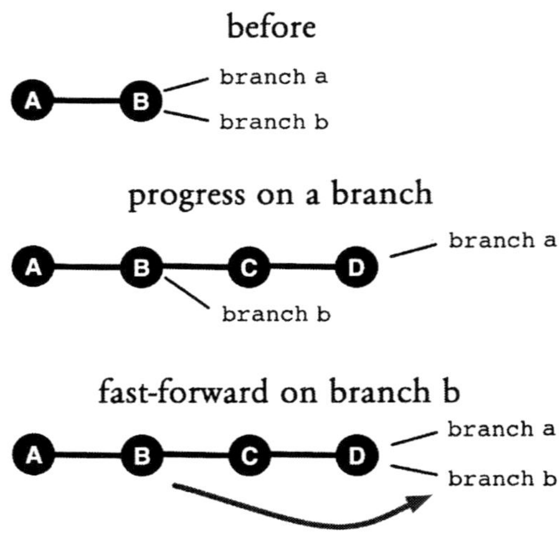

Figure 7.5: Fast-forward merge

The advantage of a fast-forward merge is that the history remains simple and linear. The disadvantage is that you cannot see in the history that a merge has occurred. Because of this disadvantage, in some workflows in this book we use the **--no-ff** option to force a new commit to occur (See Figure 7.6).

```
> git merge --no-ff a-branch
```

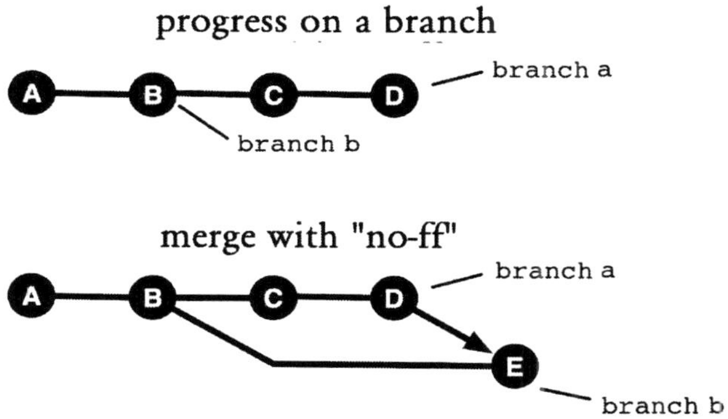

Figure 7.6: No fast-forward merge

First-Parent History

A merge commit usually has two predecessors, even though there can be more than two predecessors in an octopus merge. In the following example, there are two preceding commits **ed1c70e** and **f1d55be**.

```
> git log --merges

commit 7f3eae07c42df05f894fdd4754e38ab9e66a5051
Merge: ed1c70e f1d55be
Author: ...
```

The first specified commit in the example above (**ed1c70e**) is called the first parent. It is the commit that was HEAD when the merge was performed. This indicates where the merge has occurred.

If all developers are working on the same branch, then the result of when and where merges are performed is arbitrary. In this case, which one if the first-parent commit is rather uninteresting.

On the other hand, when developing with feature branches where one feature after another is integrated on the feature branch, the result of the integration branch (in this example, **master**) is a sequence of merge commits (See Figure 7.7). The first parent is always the merge commit of the previous feature.

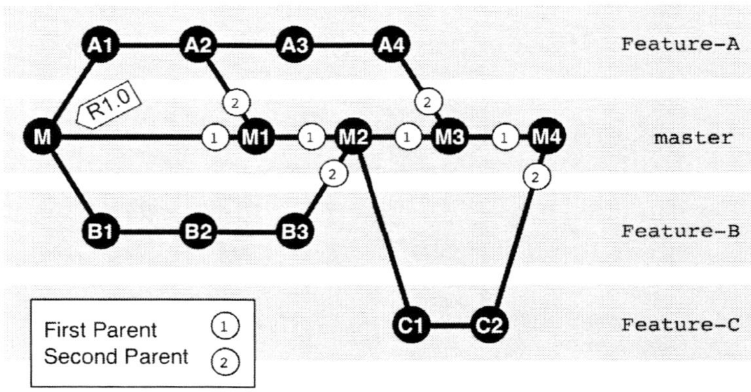

Figure 7.7: First-parent history

If you follow the first parent chain all the way down to the root, you will get an overview of the feature integrations. This episode is called the first-parent history. You can use the **--first-parent** option of the **log** command to display the feature integrations:

```
> git log --first-parent --oneline R1.0..master

7f3eae0 Merge branch 'Feature-C' Finished (M4)
ed1c70e Merge branch 'Feature-A' Finished (M3)
eeb6ec2 Merge branch 'Feature-B' Finished (M2)
8ce3213 Merge branch 'Feature-A' Partial delivery (M1)
```

The beauty of the first-parent history is that it provides a summarized presentation of the history. You can see what features have been integrated, without having to examine every single commit of the feature branches.

Attention! This only works if you do not perform any fast-forward merges on the integration branch. Otherwise, individual commits of the feature branches would be placed directly in the first-parent history of the master.

Attention! In addition, you should not perform internal merges on the integration branch (here: **master**). Instead, make sure that the features are all integrated in succession, so that you get a linear history of feature merges.

Tricky Merge Conflicts

Most Git merges are done automatically with little or no manual assistance. If two branches have evolved into very different branches, there may be tricky conflicts.

In this section we only talk about merges involving two branches. If you encounter a problem related to an octopus merge, you should cancel the merge and try to address the issue branch by branch.

The important thing is, start by collecting information to understand what is happening in the branches. Here, using the **..** notation in the **log** command might help. For example, **a..b** denotes commits from branch **b** that are not in branch **a**. It can show what "we" have done (on the current branch) that will not be listed by commits in the other branch.

```
> git log MERGE_HEAD..HEAD
```

Conversely, you can display what "the others" have done.

```
> git log HEAD..MERGE_HEAD
```

A graphical representation of branching can also be useful.

```
> git log --graph --oneline --decorate HEAD MERGE_HEAD
```

You can restrict the output of the **log** command to merge commits using the **--merge** option.

```
> git log --merge
```

Also, comparing the original version with the tips of the branches can be useful. This requires the merge base, i.e. the common ancestor of the branches in the merge.

```
> git merge-base HEAD MERGE_HEAD
ed3b1832c48b359111d00bddb071c42ba6f38324
> git diff --stat ed3b18 HEAD          % Our changes
> git diff --stat ed3b18 MERGE_HEAD    % Changes by others
```

You can also use the **difftool** command if you want to have a graphical tool instead of a text output.

Now you can see which developers are involved in the conflict. It is best if you can bring everyone to the table, then everyone can ensure that his or her changes are correctly included in the merging.

It will be harder if the others are not available, because you are not normally versed in the other branch. Technically speaking, a merge is a symmetric operation. In our mind, however, we often have an asymmetric view. You should ask yourself this question: "How do I include other people's code in my own code?" Sometimes it helps to reverse the question, taking the other's version level as a starting point, and figuring out how you would integrate your changes there. Sometimes the change of perspective helps.

Regardless, Somehow It Will Work

Pressed for time, you may be tempted to simply pick one or the other variant of the code shown by the merge tool. You should resist this temptation. If after analysis of diffs and logs and the help of the "other" versions you are still unsure how to resolve the conflict, you should cancel the merge. A few possible strategies are then:

- **Restructuring the branch:** The cleanest solution probably consists of cleaning up one of the branches by refactoring and interactive rebasing. However, this is a lot of work.

- **Merging in small steps:** If one of the two branches of finely-granular commits exists, you can proceed with one commit at a time. The advantage of this approach is that with smaller commits conflicts are usually easier to resolve. That can be time consuming if the number of commits is high, though. In any case, it is recommended that you create a local branch for this.
- **Discarding and cherry-picking:** In some cases it is better not to accept changes in an inferior branch. Some improvements can be taken with the **cherry-pick** command.
- **Rating and testing:** If the affected functionality can pass the test, you can of course try to guess when trying to resolve a conflict, and to improve the outcome until all tests pass.

Summary

- **Merge:** A merge is the merging of branches in the commit graph.
- **Merge commit:** The result of the **merge** command is a merge commit.
- **3-way merge:** Git uses the commit graph to find the last common ancestor when merging. Git then takes the changes that have taken place on a branch since the ancestor, along with the changes that have been made on the other branch. As long as the changes are happening at different code points, Git will be able to create a merge commit automatically.
- **Conflict:** A point in the code where Git cannot automatically merge, perhaps because the same line has been changed differently, is called a conflict.

- **Content conflict:** Changes often take place at different locations, but still the contents do not match. Git cannot detect such content conflicts. A project should have its own precautions, such as automated testing, in order to protect yourself from content conflicts.
- **Fast-forward merge:** It is quite common that one of the branches during a merge is the ancestor of the other branch. In this case, Git simply moves the branch pointer forward. There is no merge commit necessary.

Chapter 8 A Cleaner History with Rebasing

Many branches in a commit history are unclear. Git makes it possible to straighten out the history. The most important tool for this is the **rebase** command, which can move the impact of a commit to another place in the commit graph. You can do this,

- if you accidentally performed a commit on the wrong branch. It could be a bug fix that you have diverted to the line of development (**master**).
- when multiple developers work hard on the same software and integrate their changes frequently. Without rebasing they would create a history of many small branches and junctions (called a diamond necklace). With the **rebase** command you can instead create a smooth linear history.

The Principle: Copying of Commits

The rebasing principle is simple: Git takes a sequence of commits that you want to move, and play it again on the target branch in exactly the same order. This produces for each of the original commits a true copy of the same changeset, the same author, date and comments.

Note: At first glance it looks like Git would move commits when rebasing. In fact, the "shifted" commits are always new commits with different commit hashes. This is important if more branches have already been diverted from the original commits.

Note: As the new commits are recorded at different points in the commit graph, naturally there can be conflicts because the changes do not fit there. Such changes must then be resolved as merge conflicts manually.

Avoiding the "Diamond Chain"

When several developers working on the same software incorporate changes frequently, a commit history that looks like a diamond chain will be created. With rebasing, you can create a linear history with equivalent content.

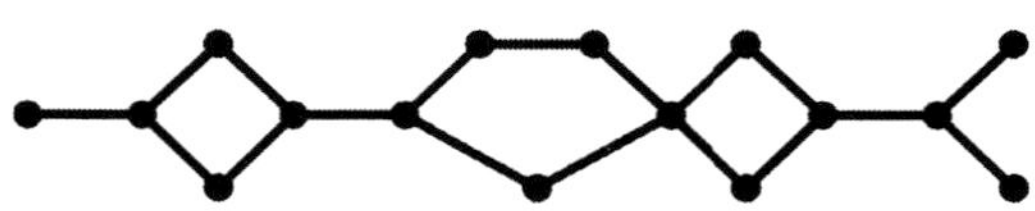

Figure 8.1: Diamond necklace

The example in Figure 8.2 shows how rebasing works. A branch called **feature-a** was diverted from the **master** branch and has two commits, **C** and **D**. At the same time, **master** has been further developed and has one more commit, **B**.

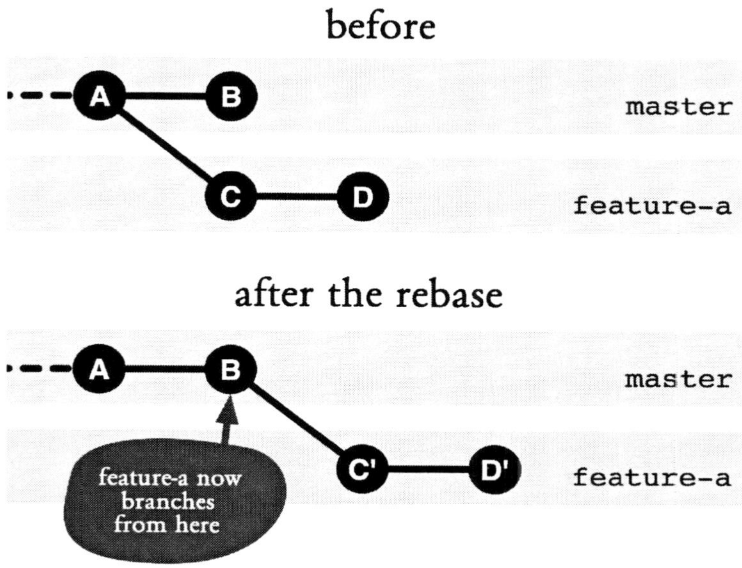

Figure 8.2: Simple rebasing

Now you can merge the changes with **git merge master** and smooth out the history again using the **rebase** command. This command takes a parameter: the branch whose latest changes will be brought into the active branch.

```
> # Branch "feature-a" is active
> git rebase master
```

Upon receiving this command, Git will rebase the active branch (**feature-a**) onto **master** by doing the following.

- **Which commits?** Git determines which commits in the active branch **feature-a** are not yet in the target branch (**master**). In our example, **C** and **D**.
- **Where?** Git determines the target commit, the commit in **master** on which **feature-a** will be rebased to. In the example, **B**.
- **Copying the commits:** Based on the target commit all changes in the commits to be rebased are replayed, creating commits **C'** and **D'**.

- **Resetting the active branch to the copy:** The active branch is moved to the top of the copied commit. In the example, **D'**.

In many cases, you should not call the **rebase** command directly. Instead, you should use the **--rebase** option with the **pull** command to rebase the changes in the remote repository.

Note: The old commits **C** and **D** are incidentally still in the repository, even though they are no longer directly visible because the branch **feature-a** is now pointing to **D'**. However, **C** and **D** can still be accessed using their hashes, respectively. Only after a garbage collection with the **gc** command will they disappear from the repository.

And When It Comes to Conflicts?

Just like the **merge** command, the **rebase** command may also terminate with conflicts when changes do not match. There is one important difference, however: When merging you get results in a single commit which are the combination of changes from both branches. When rebasing, however, several commits are generated step by step again. If everything goes smoothly, the contents of the last commit will be the same as that of the result of the **merge** command, because Git uses the same algorithms to resolve conflicts for both commands. But if the **rebase** command encounters a conflict, the process will be interrupted, with files decorated with conflict markers. You can clean up the files manually or with a merge tool, then add them to the staging area. From there you can use the **rebase** command with the **--continue** option to proceed.

```
> git add foo.txt
> git add bar.txt
> git rebase --continue
```

You can also cancel the **rebase** command using the **--abort** option. You can skip the conflicted commit using the **--skip** option. It will then simply be omitted, i.e. their changes will not appear on the new branch.

Warning! Unlike in a merge, in an interrupted rebasing parts of the copied commits may have been applied.

Transplanting A Branch

Sometimes you already created a branch and its first commit. With the **--onto** option you can transplant a branch to another location in the commit graph.

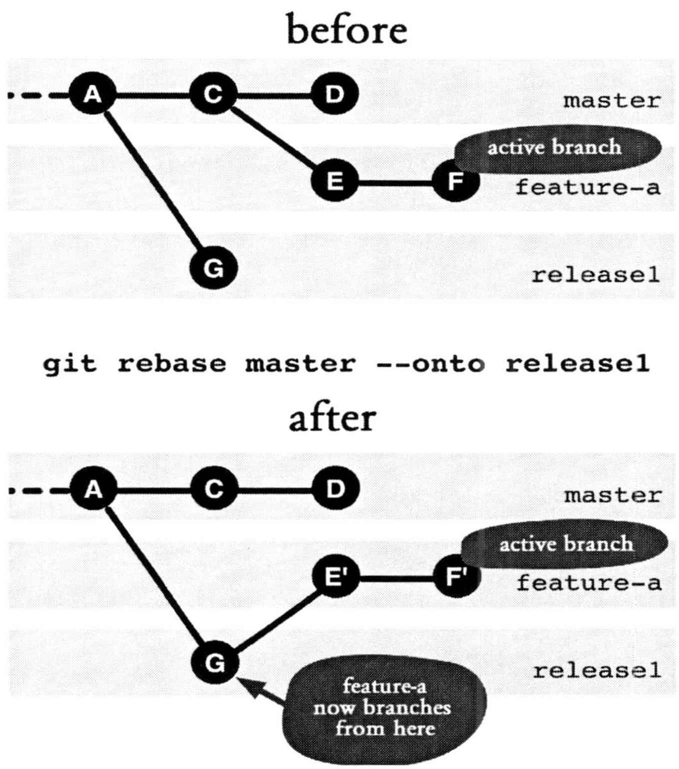

Figure 8.3: Moving a branch

In the example in Figure 8.3, the **feature-a** branch is transplanted to **release1**.

```
> # Branch "feature-a" is active
> git rebase master --onto release1
```

The first parameter to the **rebase** command specifies the original branch (in this case, **master**). Git then determines all commits in the active branch (**feature-a**) that are not in the original branch (in this example, **E** and **F**). These commits will then be copied to the location indicated by the **--onto** option (in this case, **release1**).

Step by Step
Moving a branch

A branch has to be moved to another location in the commit graph.

1 If necessary, change to the branch to be moved

```
> git checkout the-branch
```

2. Determine the origin

There is the origin branch, from which the branch to be moved has diverted. Git will move all commits that are not in the origin branch.

3. Check to see what are being moved

It is advisable to check in advance which commits will be affected, because a wrong rebasing can lead to a very confusing situation in the repository.

```
> git log origin..the-branch
```

4. Determine the target point

Choose a branch target on which the shifted branch should be rebased to.

5. Perform the rebasing

```
> git rebase origin --onto target
```

Note: The origin for the **rebase** command does not have to be a branch. It can also be any commit.

What Happens to the Original Commits after Rebasing?

Commits will be copied during rebasing. The originals (in this example, **C** and **D**) can still be accessed using their hashes. Normally, when no further branches are diverted from these commits, the next garbage collection (using the **gc** command) will simply remove them from the repository.

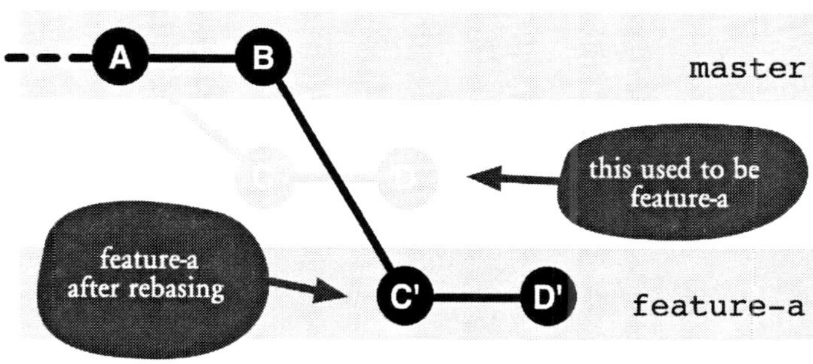

Figure 8.4: The old and new branches after rebasing

Why Is It Problematic to Have the Original and Copy Commits in the Same Repository?

Duplicates make the repository confusing. They can easily cause misunderstandings as to which branches a given code change is included in and which branches it is not included in. Normally, **git log HEAD..a-branch** shows which commits in **a-branch** are not yet in the current branch. If there are duplicates, the current branch may already contain the code change. This will complicate reviews and quality assurance.

In addition, there may be difficulties later when the branch with the duplicate commit is merged with the branch with the original commit. In the best case, Git recognizes that the same change occurred more than once, and apply them only once. In the worst case, if the duplicate commit was modified to resolve a conflict, Git does not detect this and then tried to apply the changes several times. This results in unexpected conflicts for the user.

Once you have transferred a commit to a remote repository, you should not move the commit with the **rebase** command. Otherwise, other developers could continue to work with the originals and problems will occur when it is time to merge the changes again.

Cherry-Picking

There is another way to copy a commit, namely by using the **cherry-pick** command. You specify which commit you want to have, and Git will create a new commit with the same changeset and metadata in the current branch.

```
> git cherry-pick 23ec70f6b0
```

Here are the things you should know about cherry-picking:

- **cherry-pick** does not take the history into account. **merge** and **rebase** can still classify renamed and moved files correctly. **cherry-pick** cannot.
- Cherry-picking is sometimes used to transfer small bug fixes to various release versions.
- Another application is to transfer useful changes from a feature branch that you want to remove.
- Warning: Cherry-picking can lead to the problems with duplicate commits above.

Summary

- **Rebasing:** Git can copy commits to other places in the commit graph. The changes and metadata (author, date) remain the same, but there will be a new commit hash. You can use the **rebase** command to rebuild the commit graph in many ways.
- **Just before the push:** Normally you should use the **rebase** command only on commits that have not been transferred to other repositories. Otherwise, it could later lead to nasty merge conflicts.
- **Smoothing out the history:** If you resolve conflicts during parallel development with the **merge** command, you will get a history with many branches and merges. If you use **rebase** instead of **merge**, you will get a linear history.
- **Conflicts during rebasing:** Git plays the copied commits piece by piece again. If there is a conflict because the changes do not fit the workspace, the process will be interrupted. As with **merge**, the developer can resolve the conflict manually and continue the rebasing.
- **rebase --onto:** With this option, you can move a branch to a completely different location in the commit graph.

Chapter 9 Exchanges between Repositories

Git is distributed. A repository can have many clones. Each developer has his or her own clone, maybe even several. Usually there is a project server with a central repository. This central repository represents the "official" status of a project and is also called the blessed repository. Often there are more clones, for example, for backups or on the server for continuous integration. Each clone by itself is an independent and full-fledged repository. In every clone, new commits and branches may be created. The exchange of information is therefore extremely important. For this purpose, there are **fetch**, **pull** and **push** commands.

Cloning A Repository

Repository cloning plays a major role in Git. There are many reasons to clone:

- Every developer needs at least one clone to be able to work with Git.
- Often, a clone is used as a central repository to represent the "official" status of the project.
- In multi-site development, each site will have its main clone, which is regularly compared with the major clones in other locations.

- For independent developments that take a different direction from the main project (for example, if you are planning major conversions) you often use your own clone. Such a clone is also called a fork.
- When performing tricky work on the repository that could damage the project or repository, it is often useful to create a separate clone.
- Tools for working with Git often use their own clone.
- Clones are ideal as a backup for the main repository.

The **clone** command is very easy to use. You specify the location of the original repository as a parameter and Git will create a clone in the current working directory.

Normally, right after creating a clone, Git does a checkout in the workspace. If you do not want this, you can use the **--bare** option to create a repository without a workspace. This is useful for repositories on the server side, on which a developer works directly.

How to Tell Git Where the Other Repository Is

If the other repository is local, you can simply specify the path to the directory, eg **/Users/stachi/git-book.git**. For instance, the following command clones a local repository.

```
> git clone /Users/stachi/git-book.git
```

However, if you are dealing with multiple repositories from different sources, the URL will look clearer if it is preceded by the protocol (in this case, **file**):

```
> git clone file:///Users/stachi/git-book.git
```

In addition to **file**, other protocols can also be used to access non-local repositories. The **ssh** protocol is probably the most frequently used because it enables secure authentication and the infrastructure to do so is often already in place when working with Linux or Unix servers.

```
> git clone ssh://stachi@server.de:git-book.git
```

On top of that, access is also made possible via the **http**, **https**, **ftp**, **ftps**, and **rsync** protocols or via a proprietary protocol called **git**.

Giving the Other Repository A Name

If you often access a repository, you may want to give it a name for easy access. You do this by using the **remote add** command followed by a nickname.

```
> git remote add myClone file:///tmp/git-book-clone.git
```

You can then use the short name, **myClone** in this example, instead of the repository URL with Git commands.

When cloning a repository, Git automatically stores the path to the original repository as its origin. If you call the **remote** command with the **--verbose** option, Git will list the links and show which paths were used for fetching or pushing the commits.

```
> git remote --verbose

origin ssh://stachi@server.de:git-book.git (fetch)
origin git@github.com:rpreissel/git-workflows.git (push)
klon file:///tmp/git-book-clone.git (fetch)
klon file:///tmp/git-book-clone.git (push)
```

You can delete a nickname using the **remote rm** command.

```
> git remote rm myClone
```

Fetching Data

If work continues after cloning, the original repository and the clone will drift apart. New commits as well as branches may be created in either repository.

The **fetch** command fetches commits from another repository. For each branch in the other repository, **fetch** transfers all commits that are not yet available locally,

```
> git fetch myClone
```

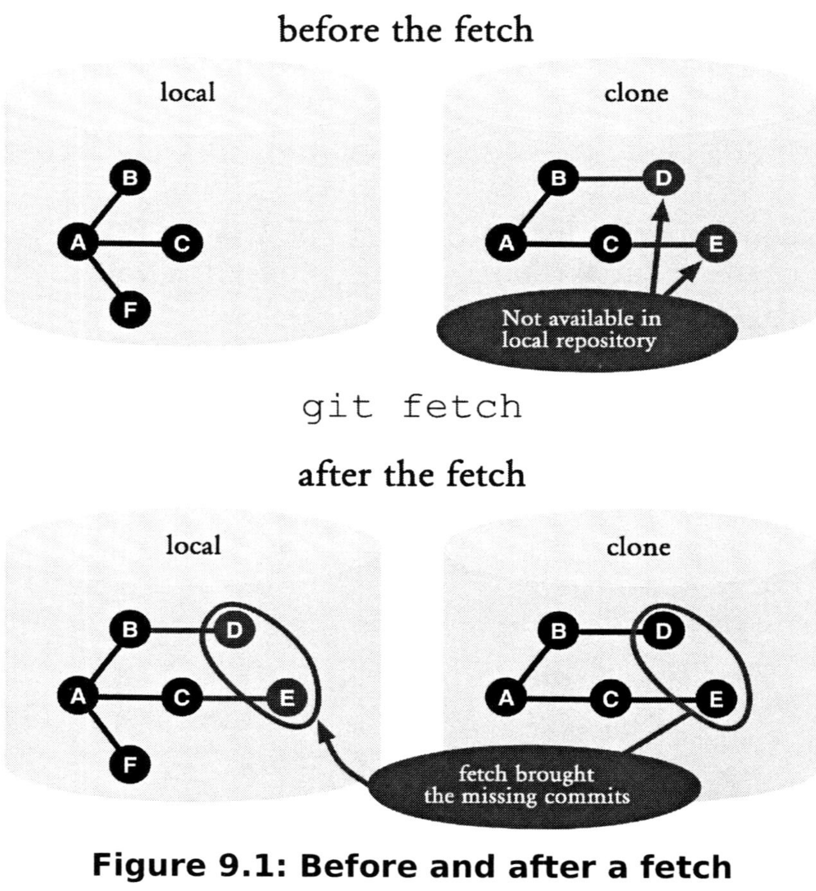

Figure 9.1: Before and after a fetch

Figure 9.1 shows what is happening here:

- **D** and **E**. The **fetch** command fetches commits that are still missing locally from the remote repository.
- **A**, **B** and **C**. Commits that are already present locally naturally are not transmitted.
- **F**. The **fetch** command operates in one direction. Commits are only transmitted from the remote repository to the local repository. To transfer local commits to the remote repository, use the **push** command.

Note that **fetch** is unidirectional. In the example, commits were transferred from the clone repository to the local repository. None of the new local commits was transferred to the clone.

You can specify a branch as a parameter to pick changes from that particular branch only. If you do not specify a parameter, **fetch** will fetch commits from all branches in the repository of origin, which is the repository from which the local repository has been cloned.

Remote-Tracking Branches: Monitoring Other Repositories

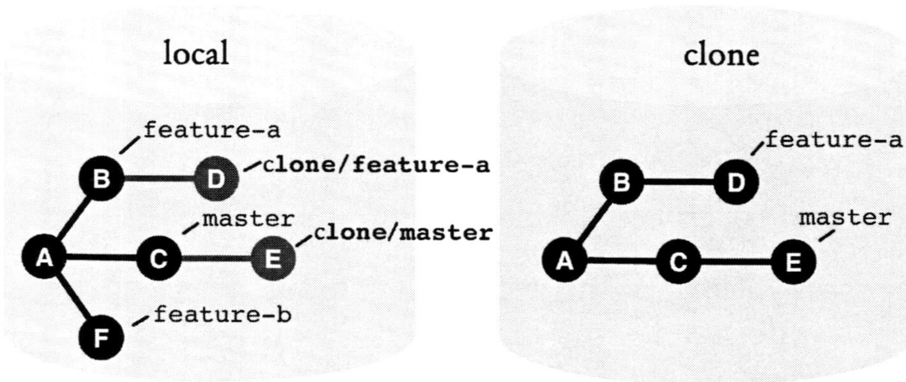

Figure 9.2: Remote-tracking branches

There are two types of branches, local and remote-tracking. You have learned about local branches, and now you will learn about remote-tracking branches too.

With a fetch, Git sets bookmarks that point to the locations of the branches in the other repository. These bookmarks are called remote tracking branches. A remote-tracking branch consists of a short name for the other repository and the name of the branch in the other repository. In Figure 9.2, **clone/feature-a** and **clone/master** are remote-tracking branches. Use the **-r** option with the **branch** command to show remote-tracking branches.

```
> git branch -r

clone/feature-a
clone/master
origin/HEAD -> origin/master
origin/feature-a
```

```
origin/master
```

You can compare your local branches with what other developers have done in the meantime. The **diff** command shows how the versions differ.

```
> git diff feature-a clone/feature-a
```

Use the **log** command to show which commits were added from the remote repository.

```
> git log --oneline feature-a..klon/feature-a
```

The next time you do a fetch, the remote-tracking branches will be updated again.

Note: Git treats remote-tracking branches differently from local branches. You can check out a remote-tracking branch just like a local one, but this puts you in a detached HEAD state (just like checking out an old commit). Instead, you should branch off a local branch from the remote-tracking branch, as described in the next section.

```
> git checkout -b feature-b clone/feature-b
```

Working with Local Branches from Other Repositories

You can also create a local branch with a fetch. To do this, use the colon (:). Specify the name of the branch from the other repository before the colon and the name of the local branch after the colon.

```
> git fetch clone feature-b:my-feature-b
```

This command fetches branch **feature-b** from repository **clone** and branches thereof. A local branch named **my-feature-b** will be created if none exists or updated if it already exists.

Pull = Fetch + Merge

A fetch often causes conflicts, because new commits have been added locally or to the other repository. In most cases, a merge is appropriate.

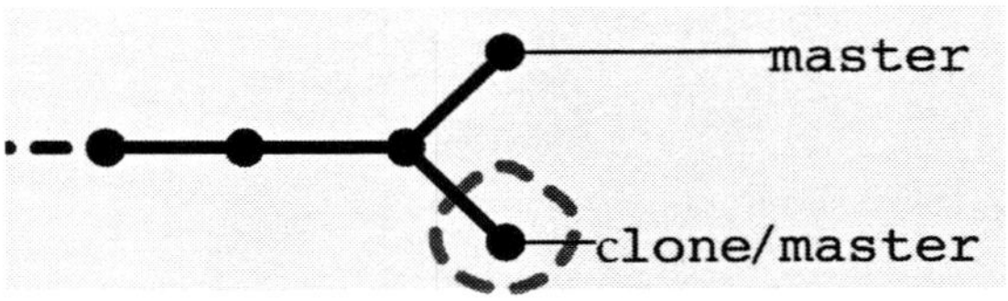

Figure 9.3: Double heads after a fetch. The commit that did not get picked up is highlighted

The **pull** command does exactly that: it imports commits from a remote repository and if necessary does a merge on the **current branch** (see Figure 9.4).

```
> git pull
```

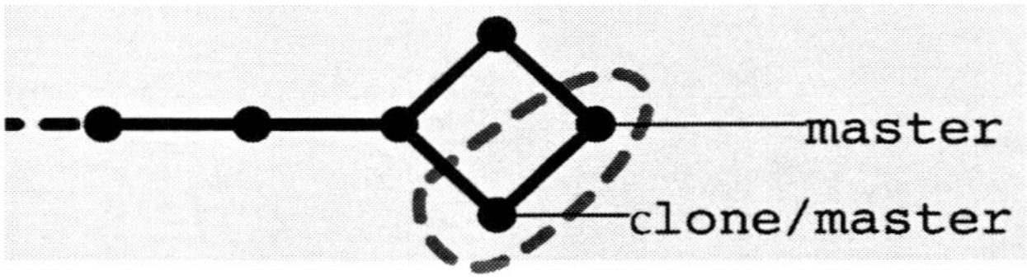

Figure 9.4: After a pull. The commit that did not get picked up and the merge commit are highlighted

For Diamond Haters: --rebase

Those who prefer a linear history can use the **pull** command with the **--rebase** option. Then, a rebasing instead of a merge will be performed (see Figure 9.5).

```
> git pull --rebase
```

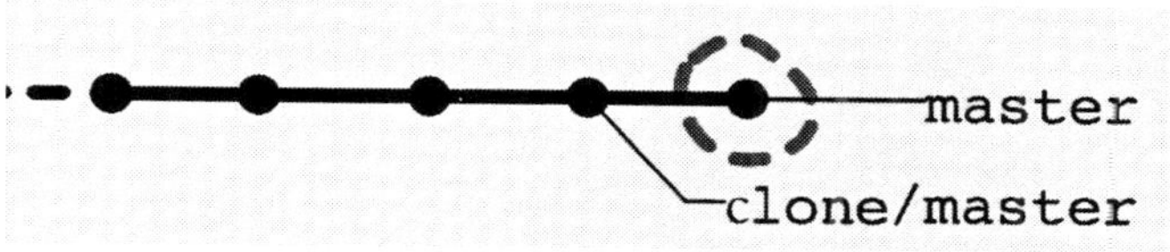

Figure 9.5: After a pull. Highlighted is the shifted commit

Push, the Opposite of Pull

You use the **push** command to transfer commits from the local repository to a remote repository. For example, the following command transfers new local commits on the **feature-a** branch to a remote repository pointed by **clone** and updates the branch pointer to **feature-a** there.

```
> git push clone feature-a
```

There are a few important differences between **push** and **pull** that you should consider:

- **Write access: push** only works if you have write access on the other repository.
- **Fast-forward only:** A push never leads to a merge (unlike the **pull** command). A push is only permitted in fast-forward settings, i.e., when no new commits have been added to the branch in the other repository.
- **No remote tracking branches**
- **Calling push without parameters:** Without parameters, **push** will only send those local branches for which there is match with the same name in the other repository. On the other hand, **pull** and **fetch** pick up all the branches.

Note that Git will refuse to push if fast-forward is not possible. You can, however, force it with the **--force** option. However, you should not do that, because this could result in a commit being lost in the other repository. It is always better to resolve conflicts locally, as described in the following step by step instructions.

Step by Step
Push denied. What next?

The reason why a push is denied is because there are already changes added to the same branch in the other repository. The conflicts must first be resolved locally before a push can pass.

1. Find the conflicts

The **push** command reports this through the following somewhat cumbersome message:

```
> git push clone feature-a

To /tmp/git-book-clone.git
! [rejected]
feature-a -> feature-a (non-fast-forward)
error: failed to push some refs to '/Users/stachi/Book/'
To prevent you from losing history, non-fast-forward updates
were
rejected. Merge the remote changes (e.g. 'git pull') before
pushing
again. See the 'Note about fast-forwards' section of
'git push --help' for details.
```

2. Change branch

```
> git checkout feature-a
```

3. Do a pull

```
> git pull
```

4. If necessary, clean up merge conflicts

```
> git mergetool

> git commit --all
```

```
checkout feature-a
```

5. Push once again

```
> git push clone feature-a
```

If you called **push** with no parameters, you may have to run the above steps several times, once for each branch with conflicts.

Naming Branches

It is often advisable to agree on uniform branch names when working together in a software team.

Git gives the developer the freedom to name local branches. If you do this, you must use the colon in the parameters for **fetch**, **pull** or **push**. The word before the colon specifies the source branch and the word after the colon specifies the target branch. Consider the following example.

```
> git pull clone feature-a:favorite-feature
```

Here, **pull** imports the **feature-a** branch in repository **clone** and locally names the branch **favorite-feature**.

Deleting a branch in a remote repository is a special case. In this case, you use the **push** command with a colon and leave the left side of the colon empty, implying setting the branch in question to nothing.

Step by Step
Deleting a branch in a remote repository
You want to delete a branch in a remote repository. Warning: the following steps may cause commits to be lost.

1. Delete a branch in a remote repository

Pay attention to the colon.

```
> git push clone :feature-a
```

2. If necessary, delete the local branch

```
> git branch -d feature-a
```

Summary

- **Repository URLs:** The location of a remote repository can be specified in URL format, e.g. **ssh://stachi@server.de:git-book.git**. The following protocols are supported: **file**, **ssh**, **http**, **https**, **ftp**, **ftps**, **rsync** and **git**.
- **Nicknames:** You can define a nickname for a repository with the **remote** command, so you do not have to specify the long URL every time you need to access the repository.
- **Fetch:** The **fetch** command fetches commits on branches from a remote repository. Of course, it will only transfer commits that are not locally available yet.
- **Fetch without parameters:** Retrieves the commits for all branches in the remote repository.
- **Fetch without moving local branches:** This will only fetch commits and then set remote-tracking branches.

- **Remote-tracking branches:** You indicate the location of branches in remote repositories, e.g. **clone/feature-a**. The **fetch** and **pull** commands update the remote tracking branches.
- **Pull = fetch + merge:** The **pull** command is a combination of two operations. It first does a fetch. Thereafter, it merges the local changes in the currnet branch with changes that have been retrieved from the remote repository.
- **Push:** The **push** command transfers commits in local branches to a remote repository.
- **Push transfers branches:** Branch pointers are set in the remote repository. These are set to the state of the local repository.
- **Push fast-forward only!** Git will reject a push if another developer has done a push on the same branch, such that fast-forward is not possible. In this case, the changes must first be brought together locally, for example by using a pull.
- **Push without parameters:** In this case, only local branches with identically named matches in the remote repository will be transferred.

Chapter 10
Version Tagging

Most projects use numbers or names to identify software versions, such as 1.7.3.2 or "gingerbread." In Git you can use tags.

Creating A Tag

Step by Step
Tagging a commit

1. Creating a normal tag
In the following example, we will create a tag named **1.2.3.4** with comment "Freshly built." for the current version of the **master** branch.

```
> git tag 1.2.3.4 master -m "Freshly built."
```

2. Push: a single tag
A push does not automatically transfer tags. However, if you explicitly specify a tag name, it will be transferred.

```
> git push origin 1.2.3.4
```

Using the **--tags** option with the **push** command will also push the tags for the transferred branch.

```
> git push --tags
```

If you use GnuPG (Gnu Privacy Guard), you can provide tags with a digital signature by using the **-s** option. The prerequisite is that you have entered a default email address in Git and the email address must also be a registered user ID in GnuPG.

```
> git tag 1.2.3.4 master -s -m "Signed."
```

Attention! If you create a tag with the **-m**, **-a**, **-s** or **-u** option, Git will create a tag as a separate object in the repository. This object will contain information about the user and the time it was created. Without these options, Git will only create a so-called lightweight tag that only recognizes the commit hash.

Which Tags Are There?

If you call the **tag** command without parameters, you will see the list of all tags. This can be a long list, and you can use the **-l** option with a pattern like **1.2.*** to reduce the output.

```
> git tag -l 1.2.*

1.2.0.0       Beginning.
   ...
1.2.3.3       New build.
1.2.3.4       Recently built.
```

Printing the Tag Hashes

The **show-ref** command with the **--tags** option lists the commit hashes of the tag objects. You can use the **-dereference** option to also print the hash of the commit objects, marked with **^{}**.

```
> git show-ref --dereference --tags

...
f63cd7181787c9973788a97648796468cec474aa refs/tags/1.2.3.3
cef89bbd7121aac3cc38fe3a342045c9401bd6b9 refs/tags/1.2.3.3^{}
```

```
4a0228bdd0ab5e0180422c82bf706c42671a81af refs/tags/1.2.3.4
cef89bbd7121aac3cc38fe3a342045c9401bd6b9 refs/tags/1.2.3.4^{}
```

Adding Tags to the Log Output

Using the **--decorate** option with the **log** command prints the tags and branches of each commit.

```
> git log --oneline --decorate
```

```
cef89bb (HEAD, tag: 1.2.3.4) Again, everything rebuilt.
9d4caed Merge branch 'Other'.
dcd1c6c Changed.
cce1a68 (tag: 1.2.3.3) Something changed
```

In What Version Is It in?

Often the question arises whether a particular feature or bug fix is already included in the version that has been installed by a customer. If the commit is known, the question is easy to answer. The **--contains** option of the **tag** command lists all the tags in the history that contains the commit.

```
> git tag --contains f63cd71
```

```
1.2.3.3
1.2.3.4
```

Attention! The result can be misleading if some commits have been copied. For example, if versions are put together through cherry-picking, it is tricky to figure out whether the change is included. You could log for a particular tag after the commit comment search.

```
> git log --oneline 1.2.3.3 | grep "a comment."
```

However, this only works if you have added comments that identify the changes, either by using a meaningful description or a ticket ID from the bug tracking system. This is another good reason to avoid copying commits.

How to Change A Tag?

It is best not to change it. In Git, a tag is provided as a permanent marker for a version. As long as you have not transferred it with a push to another repository, you can change a tag by recreating it with the **--force** option. If the tag is already widespread, it can cause confusion if a second variant is circulated.

When Do I Need A Floating Tag?

If you need a movable marker, say for the status, which is currently installed in production, just take a branch.

Summary

- **Create a tag:** This is done with the **tag** command.
- **Push:** The **push** command only transfers tags that you specify explicitly, for example **git push origin 1.2.3.4**, unless you use the **--tags** option.
- **Pull and fetch:** The **pull** and **fetch** commands fetch all the tags from the affected branches automatically, unless you use **--no-tags**.
- **Show all tags:** This can be done with **git tag -l**.
- **Show tags in the log:** You can use **git log --decorate**.
- **Shared commit in tag:** To inquire if a tag contains a commit, use the **tag** command with the **--contains** option.

- **Floating tags do not exist:** In Git tags are permanent markers that you should not alter after they were created. If you need to change a tag, you just take a branch.

Chapter 11 Dependencies between Repositories

In Git the repository is the release unit, in the sense that a version, branch and tag can only be created on a whole repository. If a project contains subprojects that each has its own release cycle and thus its own versions, there must also be a repository for each subproject.

The relationship between the main project and the sub-projects can be implemented with Git **submodule** or **subtree** command.

Note

The **subtree** command is first officially included in Git in version 1.7.11. However, it is only an optional component located under the **contrib** directory. Some Git installation packages include the **subtree** command automatically, others require manual installation.

The main difference between the submodule and subtree concepts is that with submodules the main repository only references the module repositories, whereas with subtree the contents of the module repositories are imported into the main repository.

Dependencies with Submodules

With submodules, a module repository can be embedded into the main repository. For this purpose, a directory with a commit in a module repository will be linked to the main repository.

Figure 11.1 shows the basic structure. There are two repositories: **main** and **sub**. In the main repository, the **sub** directory will be linked with the module repository. In the workspace of the main repository there is a complete module repository under the **sub** directory. The actual main repository will only reference the module repository. For this purpose, there is a file named **.gitmodules**, in which the absolute path to each module repository is defined.

```
[submodule "sub"]
path = sub
url = /project/sub
```

In addition to the **.gitmodules** file, the references to submodules are also stored in the **.git/config** file. This is done when you call the **submodule init** command, which reads the **.gitmodules** file and writes the information in the **.git/config** file. This indirect configuration allows the paths to the module repositories to be adjusted locally in the **.git/config** file.

```
[core]
repositoryformatversion = 0
filemode = true
bare = false
logallrefupdates = true
ignorecase = true
[submodule "sub"]
url = /project/sub
```

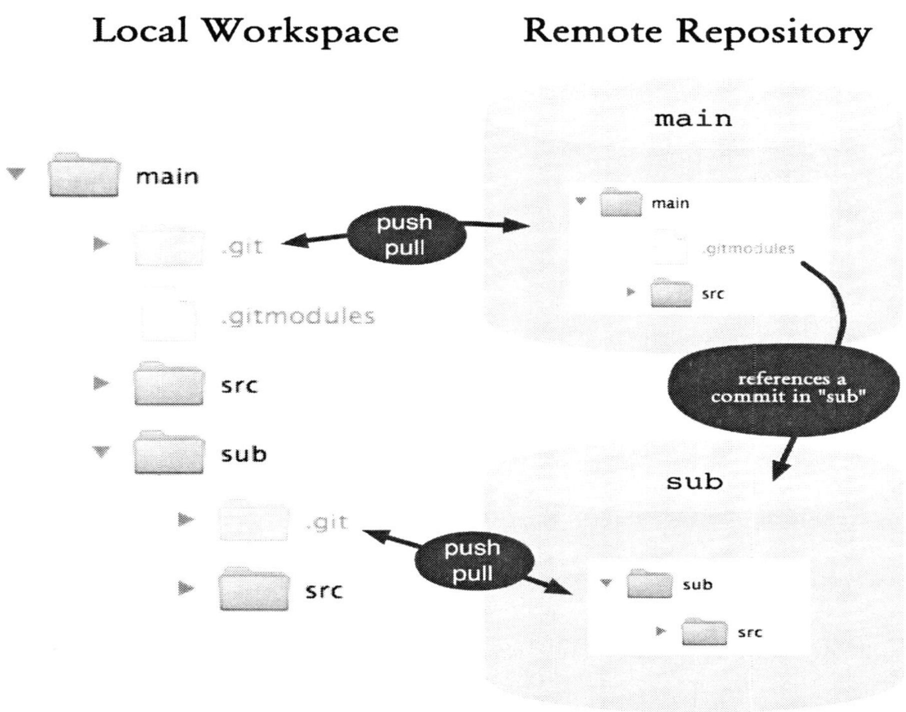

Figure 11.1: The fundamentals of submodules

With the previous information it would not be possible for each commit in the main repository to reproduce the corresponding version of the module repository. As such, the commit in the module repository is still needed. This will be stored in the object tree in the main repository. The following is the object tree. The third entry, **sub**, is a submodule, which can be recognized by its **commit** type. The hash that follows references the commit in the module repository.

```
100644 blob 1e2b1d1d51392717a479eaaaa79c82df1c35d442    .gitmodules
100644 tree 19102815663d23f8b75a47e7a01965dcdc96468c    src
160000 commit 7fa7e1c1bd6c920ba71bd791f35969425d28b91b  sub
```

Step by Step
Embedding a submodule

An existing Git project is embedded as a submodule in a different project.

1. Link the directory

To include a submodule, you have to use the **submodule add** command and pass the absolute path to the module repository and the directory name:

```
> git submodule add /global-path-to/sub sub
```

As a result, the module repository is completely cloned into the specified directory (it creates its own **.git** directory). In addition, the **.gitmodules** file in the main repository is created or updated.

2. Register the submodule in config

In addition, the new submodule has to be registered in the **.git/config** file. This is done by using the **submodule init** command.

```
> git submodule init
```

3. Select the submodule version

The workspace of the module repository is initially set to the HEAD of the default branch. To use another commit in the submodule, use the **checkout** command and select the appropriate version:

```
> cd sub
> git checkout v1.0
```

4. Add the .gitmodules file and subdirectories to the commit

When you add a submodule, the **.gitmodules** file will be created or updated and must be added to the commit. In addition, the new directory of the submodule must also be added:

```
> cd ..
> git add .gitmodules
> git add sub
```

5. Do a commit
Finally, you need to do a commit in the main repository.

```
> git commit -m "Submodule added"
```

If a repository that contains submodules is cloned, you must call the **submodule init** command. This command will transfer the URLs of the submodules in the **.git/config** file. Subsequently, calling the **submodule update** command will clone the directories of the module repositories.

Step by Step
Cloning a project with submodules

When you clone a repository that contains a submodule, initially only the main repository will be created in the workspace. The submodule must be explicitly initialized and updated.

1. Initialize the submodule
First, you must register the submodule using the **submodule init** command:

```
> git submodule init
```

2. Update the submodule
After the submodule is initialized in the Git configuration, you can use the **submodule update** command to completely download the submodule:

```
> git submodule update
```

You can view the hash of a referenced commit in a submodule using the **submodule status** command. Any tag will be shown in brackets at the end of the output.

```
> git submodule status
```

```
091559ec65c0ded42556714c3e6936c3b1a90422 sub (v1.0)
```

Git always refers to exactly one commit in the module repository. Meanwhile the commit hash is also part of every commit in the main repository. It follows that new commits in the module repository are not automatically recorded in the main repository. This behavior is explicitly intended, so that you have to obtain the matching project version in the module repository when restoring a project version in the main repository.

Step by Step
Using a new version in the submodule

There is a new version of the submodule that should be used. What do you do?

1. Update the submodule

First, bring the local workspace of the submodule to the desired state. Typically, you would start with a **fetch** command to get the latest commit in the module repository.

```
> cd sub
> git fetch
```

Next, specify the desired commit with the **checkout** command.

```
> git checkout v2.0
```

2. Use the new version

Finally, prepare the new commit in the submodule directory and do a commit.

```
> cd ..
> git add sub
> git commit -m "New version of the submodule"
```

If you intend to use a new version of the module repository in the main repository, you have to explicitly change this.

If you are working in the main repository and at the same time working in the module repository, then you have to commit changes to both repositories. If you have a central repository, both repositories must be transmitted separately using the **push** command.

Step by Step
Working with submodules

In a workspace files in the main repository and files in the module repository have been changed. The main repository should then point to the new commit in the module repository.

1. Commit and push changes in the module repository

First, the changes in the module repository are completed with a commit and possibly transmitted with the push command to the central repository:

```
> cd sub
> git add foo.txt
> git commit -m "Changed submodule"
> git push
```

2. Commit and push changes in the main repository

Next, changes in the main repository, including the reference to the new commit in the module repository, are committed and, if necessary, transferred:

```
> cd ..
> git add bar.txt
> git add sub
> git commit -m "New version of submodule"
```

After every update to a workspace that contains submodules, you should call the **submodule update** command to get the correct versions of the submodules.

If an entirely new submodule has been added, then before calling the **submodule update** command you should call **submodule init**.

As a developer, it is good enough if you run the init-update sequence after each update to the workspace (checkout, merge, rebase, reset, pull).

Step by Step
Updating a submodule

If a new version of a submodule was recorded by another developer, then you should update your own local clone and workspace.

```
> git submodule init

> git submodule update

From /project/sub
   091559e..4722848   master       -> origin/master
 * [new tag]          v1.0         -> v1.0
 * [new tag]          v2.0         -> v2.0
Submodule path 'sub':
checked out '472284843ce4c0b0bb503bc4921ab7...1e51'
```

The **submodule init** command transfers information from the **.gitmodules** file to the **.git/config** file only if there is no corresponding entry for the module. As such, the paths to the module repository can be adjusted locally. However, if another developer changed the official path of the **.gitmodules** file, the change will not be accepted. The **submodule sync** command does exactly this task. It updates the paths in the **.git/config** file and overwrites any local changes.

Dependencies with Subtrees

With subtrees, module repositories can be embedded into a Git repository. For this purpose, a directory in the repository is associated with a commit, a tag or a branch in a module repository. Unlike submodules, however, the entire content of an embedded module repository is imported and not just referenced in the main repository. This makes the main directory self-sufficient to work against.

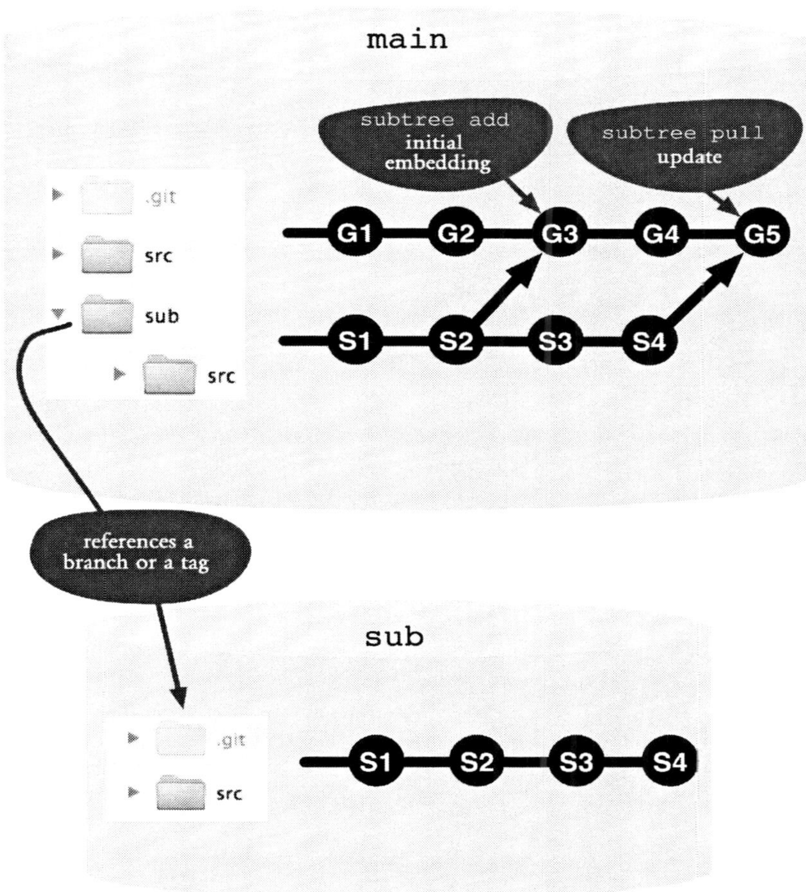

Figure 11.2: The fundamentals of subtree

Figure 11.2 shows the basic structure. There are two repositories: **main** and **sub**. The **sub** directory in the main directory is linked with the module directory (using the **subtree add** command). In the main repository, under the **sub** directory, there are files from a version of the module repository.

Technically, the **subtree add** command imports all commits from the module repository to the main repository (See commits **S1** and **S2**). Then, the current branch of the main repository is linked with the specified commit in the module repository (See merge commit **G3**). Internally, the subtree merge strategy (**--strategy=subtree**) is used. This results in a merge in the specified directory, so that the content of the module repository lands under the **sub** directory.

Step by Step
Embedding a subtree

To embed a module repository, you have to add it to the main repository using the **subtree add** command. (You only have to call **subtree add** once.) In this case, the subdirectory is specified as **--prefix**. In addition, the URL of the module repository and the desired tag or branch must also be specified:

```
> git subtree add --prefix=sub /global-path-to/sub v2.0
```

If the module repository's history is not relevant in the context of the main repository, you can use the **--squash** option to only fetch the contents of the specified commit.

```
> git subtree add --squash --prefix=sub /global-path-to/sub
    master
```

As a result, a new merge commit is created and its hash added as a comment, so that the correct module commit can be fetched at the next update.

Unlike submodules, when cloning a repository that has subtrees, there is nothing special to be observed. The normal **clone** command will pick up the main repository and all the module repositories it contains.

```
> git clone /path-to/main
```

Step by Step
Using a new version of subtree

There is another version of an embedded subtree to be used.

The **subtree pull** command updates an embedded subtree. The same parameters used for **subtree add** can be used for **subtree pull**. If a tag has been used with an add, a new tag must be used. If a branch was used, the same branch or a different branch can be specified. If there are no changes to the branch, **subtree pull** will do nothing.

```
> git subtree pull --prefix=sub /global-path-to/sub v2.1
```

Also, by using the **--squash** option with a pull, you can skip the module repository's history. In this case, no intermediate commits will be brought, only the one specified. You can also use the **--squash** option to return to an older version of the module repository, eg from v2.0 to v1.5.

```
> git subtree pull --squash --prefix=sub /global-path-to/sub
    master
```

Also with subtrees, it is possible to make changes in the embedded module directories. Here, nothing special needs to be done. You simply use the normal **commit** command. You can version changes in the main repository and one or more module directories in one commit.

Only when retransmitting the module changes in the respective repository do you need to take special precautions.

Step by Step
Propagating changes in a module repository

Changes in module directories are to be transferred to a module repository.

1. Separate changes in the module directory
First, use the **subtree split** command to separate changes in the module directory from other changes. This command will generate, based on the last known module repository commit, a new commit for each commit in which a module file has been changed. The result is a local branch which points to the new commits (for example, **sub/master**). If you do not use **squash** with the **subtree add** and **subtree pull** commands, use the **--rejoin** option. This will simplify the repeated invocation of **split**:

```
> git subtree split --rejoin --prefix sub --branch sub/master
```

2. Merge changes with the module repository
The local changes must be merged with the remote changes in the module repository. Therefore, first activate the newly created branch and then retrieve the latest version of the target branch. Afterward, both branches must be merged.

```
> git checkout sub/master
> git fetch /global-path-to/sub master
> git merge FETCH_HEAD
```

Note that the fetch with a URL creates a temporary reference **FETCH_HEAD**, which points to the most recent commit of the fetched branch. If you are working with a remote branch, you can of course use the remote name instead of the URL. After that, the target branch will be directly available, not only **FETCH_HEAD**.

3. Transfer changes to the module repository and delete the temporary branch
The local changes in the temporary branch must be pushed to the remote module repository. You can then switch back to the branch in the main repository and delete the temporary branch:

```
> git push /global-path-to/sub HEAD:master
> git checkout master
> git branch -d sub/master
```

As can be clearly seen from the above, most subtree operations are simpler than those of submodules. Only extracting the changes is similarly complex.

In many scenarios, however, no extraction is required, as you would work in the main repository and not in the module directory.

Summary

- **Embed a submodule:** Use the **submodule add** and **submodule init** commands to embed a submodule.
- **Clone a project that contains submodules:** After cloning the project, use the **submodule init** and **submodule update** commands.
- **Select a new version of a submodule:** First, select the new commit in the submodule directory (using the **checkout** command). Then, do a commit in the main repository.
- **Handle the module repository and main repository simultaneously:** it must be carried out with the commit in the module repository first and then with the commit in the main repository. Both

repositories must be pushed separately with the **push** command.

- **Embed a subtree:** Use the **subtree add** command to embed a subtree.
- **Select a new version of the subtree:** The **subtree pull** command updates the module directory to the desired branch or tag.
- **Extract changes in the module directory:** The **subtree split** command creates a separate branch that includes the changes in the module directory. Using the **merge** command, these changes can then be merged with the other changes and pushed using the **push** command.

Chapter 12
Tips and Tricks

We did not want to overload the introductory chapters and limited ourselves to the essential concepts and typical applications. In this chapter, however, you will find a collection of tips and tricks, some of which can be very helpful in certain situations but you or others might never need. Probably it is sufficient if you skim this chapter briefly so you know what is here. You can look up the details if you need them.

Don’t Panic, There Is A Reflog!

Git is like a dog. It can smell your fear.

I smiled when I saw this saying in my twitter timeline. Git is actually somewhat intimidating to beginners. But if Git is really a dog, then it is probably a herding dog trying to protect its (developer) herd.

You should know that Git does not immediately delete objects in the repository. Whenever you change something, Git creates new objects in the repository; the old ones are not deleted. Even garbage collection, for example by using the **gc** command, only deletes objects with a certain minimum age. The default setting for this is two weeks (configuration option: **gc.pruneexpire**).

In addition, Git keeps track of all changes in a branch. This so-called reflog resides in the **.git/logs** directory. With the **--walk-reflogs** option, the **log** command can display the local history of a branch.

```
> git log --walk-reflogs mybranch
```

If you can find the commit that contains the "lost" changes, then you can bring back the changes again, for example by using the **cherry-pick** command, the **rebase** command or with a simple merge.

Attention! For local clones the reflog is normally active. Bare repositories that you normally puts on servers, however, do not have the reflog by default. You can turn it on using this command:

```
> git config core.logAllRefUpdates true
```

It may be useful to make it a system-wide default setting:

```
> git config --system core.logAllRefUpdates true
```

Ignoring Local Changes Temporarily

Sometimes you change files that are managed by Git and that you do not want to include in versioning. An example: When writing this book, we often commented out chapters so that we can complete the document faster. Naturally, we did not want these changes to be versioned. Another example: To find an error, you generate extra debugging information, which will no longer be needed later.

Entries in **.gitignore** do not help here, because they only work on files that are not yet managed by Git. You can work around the problem by using selective commits. However, this is a bit tedious because then you have to choose again for each subsequent commit, what changes you do and do not want to accept.

Step by Step
Ignoring versioned files

Git-managed files are temporarily ignored, so that changes to these files will not be accepted.

1. Ignore versioned files

The **--assume-unchanged** option of the **update-index** command creates a mark in the staging area to ensure that Git will no longer checks whether the specified file has changed, and simply pretends that the file is unchanged.

```
> git update-index --assume-unchanged foo.txt
```

2. Resume work

Now you can resume work. The **status** and **add** commands will not show changes to the **foo.txt** file.

3. Stop ignoring

You can use **--no-assume-unchanged** to cancel the effect of **--assume-unchanged** for individual files. Using **--really-refresh** you can reset the status for all files.

```
> git update-index --really-refresh
```

Examining Changes to Text Files

The normal Git diff algorithm compares two files line by line. In your source code, you often change single lines without touching the neighboring lines, which means differences can be easily noticed with diff. In text files, however, it is a different story. Changes are often wrapped, i.e. words move from one line to another. From the output of diff, it is hard to see what exactly has changed in a text file.

```
> git diff

...
-Walter goes every
-day to schiil.
+Walter goes to
+school.
...
```

For continuous text, the **--word-diff** option can help as it can show changes word by word.

```
> git diff --word-diff

  ...
Walter goes [-every -]
[-day] to
[-schiil.-]{+school.+}
  ...
```

With **--word-diff=color** you can have the differences highlighted in a different color.

alias - Shortcuts for Git Commands

If you use Git from the command line often, it may be useful to define shortcuts for frequently used commands.

```
> git config --global alias.ci commit

> git config --global alias.st status
```

Here we set up aliases **ci** and **st** for commit and status, respectively. They can be used immediately. For example:

```
> git st
```

Aliases are also considered in Git tab completion (if installed). Therefore, it may also be useful to set up aliases for rarely used commands. For example:

```
> git config --global alias.ignore-temporarily
    'update-index --assume-unchanged'
```

Branches as Temporary Pointers to Commits

If you are looking for errors or trying to fix tricky merge conflicts, you might often remember relevant commits, for example a point where everything was still good, or a merge base. You may start by listing commit hashes on a piece of paper, but you should not do this! You can easily create a branch, once you discover a commit of interest.

```
> git branch tmp/a-silly-error 8b167
```

From now on you can refer to the commit by name. The tab completion now "knows" that name. You can, for instance, inquire which tags contain the commit in question.

```
> git tag --contains tmp/a-silly-error

1.0.2
1.0.3
```

The following command creates a branch named **tmp/merge-base** as a pointer to the merge base of the **master** and **feature** branches.

```
> git branch tmp/merge-base
        'git merge-base master feature'
```

The **tmp/** prefix is a naming convention: This is a namespace for temporary branches, to make it easier to distinguish them from normal branches. It is not a technical requirement. You can call the temporary branches whatever you want.

Later you can clear the branches using the following command.

```
> git branch -D
    'git branch --no-color --list tmp/\*
    | grep -v '* '
    | xargs'
```

Moving Commits to Another Branch

When you are making changes, it is of course best to do it on the right branch. But sometimes you make a mistake and do it on the wrong branch. In such a case, you will have to move some commits to another branch.

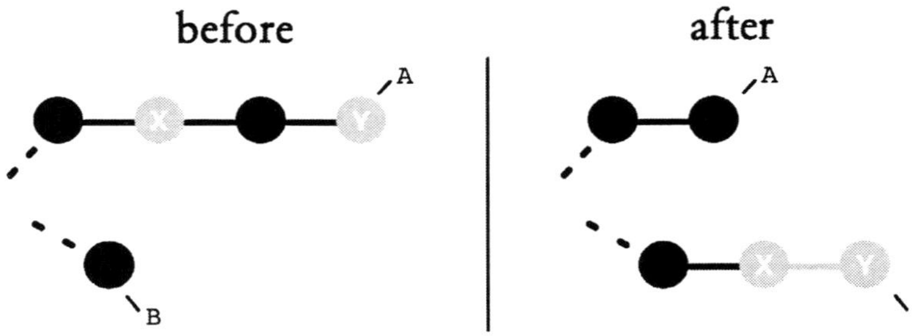

Figure 12.1: Moving commits from branch A to B

Step by Step
Moving commits to another branch

Some commits from branch **A** must be moved to branch **B**.

1. Reorder the commits and mark the dividing point with tmp/SPLIT

In order to be moved, commits must be at the end of a branch.

```
> git rebase --interactive
```

In the editor you sort the rows so that on top are rows that will remain in **A**, and at the bottom are rows that are to be moved to **B**. In between, you create a temporary branch **tmp/SPLIT** using the **exec** command. This temporary branch marks the point of separation.

```
pick 6a2f459 should stay in A 1
pick 05c2935 should stay in A 2
exec git branch -f tmp/SPLIT
```

```
pick af22ed6 should go to B 1
pick 4f30adf should go to B 2
```

The **tmp/SPLIT** branch now points to the last commit that should remain in A.

2. Do the transfer
First, create a temporary branch named **tmp/MOVE** and move it. Next, transfer **tmp/MOVE** to **B** using the **merge** command. Finally, the remaining commits are truncated to **A**.

```
> git checkout -B tmp/MOVE A
> git rebase tmp/SPLIT --onto B

> git checkout B
> git merge --ff tmp/MOVE

> git branch --force A tmp/SPLIT
```

Attention! Moving commits can confuse other developers. You should either move only commits that you have not shared with other developers, or you have to inform the other developers about it and ask them in turn to move commits that were developed on top of the moved commits.

Chapter 13 Introduction to Workflows

In the previous chapters, you learned the basic concepts of Git. Only the most important commands with the most important parameters were given.

Even with this selection you have perhaps asked the question: When will I use merge or rebase again?

You have surely searched the internet and come across various applications and even more commands and parameters. This flexibility is both a strength of Git and its weakness.

The following workflows describe typical uses of Git in development projects. Here, the focus is on completing tasks rather than on more parameters. Each of the workflows is described using only one solution. It is explained in detail so that the workflow is sufficient for your work and you do not need to always look up the help file.

Even after many years of using Git, there are tasks that need to be done less often, such as splitting a repository. In this case, the workflows can serve as a brief description of commands.

Even more lesser known commands and parameters are used in the workflows if the tasks require it. Therefore, you will also learn more ways of doing things in Git.

When Can I Use These Workflows?

When selecting a workflow selection, we looked at a typical project process.

The Beginning of the Project

If you are starting a new project from scratch and have decided to use Git as the version control, then your first task will be to choose and setup the infrastructure for versioning. The workflow "Project Setup" in Chapter 14 describes the process.

If it is a project that needs to be migrated to an existing Git project, then look at Chapter 15, "Developing on the Same Branch."

The Development

Once the infrastructure has been defined, the handling of branches should be made clear with the team. It is either all developers work on the same branch, as explained in the workflow "Developing on the Same Branch," or a separate feature branch is created for every task as explained by the workflow "Developing with Feature Branches" in Chapter 16.

If errors that were not present in earlier versions suddenly appear in development, then the workflow in Chapter 17, "Troubleshooting with Bisection" may help find the root of the problem.

For quality assurance after changes, you should set up automatic builds and tests. For working with Git in a build server, see the workflow "Working with a build server" in Chapter 18.

If Git is not yet used as the version control in your project, but you still want to work with Git, then refer to the workflow “Using other version control systems in parallel" in Chapter 19.

Project Delivery

After the development of the current release is complete, you should make sure a well tested product is delivered to the customer. At the same time, prepare for the next release and resolve problems not yet resolved in the last release. The workflow “Delivering a release” in Chapter 19 discusses it.

Refactoring

Project requirements change with time and with new insights. So it may happen that a decision to divide a project into multiple Git repositories must be reconsidered.

A monolithic project that was initially small may grow and must be modularized. The workflow “Splitting a big project” in Chapter 20 describes how a large repository can be divided into smaller ones.

The opposite can also happen. Dealing with a split in a many-repository project may turn out to be too complex. Re-merging repositories is discussed in the workflow “Merging smaller projects” in Chapter 21.

When a project has been there for a long time and undergone many changes, its associated repository may have grown very large. The histories of all the files include files that were in the local workspace of each of the developers. In particular, when large binary files have been versioned in earlier versions, this can lead to unnecessary resource consumption. The workflow “Outsourcing long histories" (in Chapter 21) describes how a project history can be split and only the more recent versions stored locally by each developer.

Structure of the Workflows

The following is the structure of the descriptions of the workflows in the following chapters. Each section is kept brief.

The entry

Each workflow begins with a brief motivation that explains why and in what context the workflow should be applied. The central tasks of the possible decisions and the special features are described. At the end there is a brief summary of the points that are discussed in this workflow. After this section you will know whether or not the workflow is relevant for your project.

The Overview

This section describes the basic procedures by way of an example. It describes the basic terms, concepts, and Git commands that are needed in this workflow.

After this section you will understand how the workflow works in principle and what Git resources are used.

The Requirements

Each workflow works only under certain conditions. After this section you will learn if the workspace can be used in your project. You will recognize what prerequisites need to be provided or why this workflow cannot be applied.

The Compact Workflow

This brief overview describes the workflow in a few sentences and presents the main concepts and ideas. If you use this book as a reference, this page will serve as a reminder.

Process and Implementation

A workflow may consist of one or more processes. Processes describe individual subtasks that you need to carry out to complete a task. This section describes each process in detail as well as which Git commands must be run with what parameters and in what order. It is deliberately written as a proposed implementation.

After this section you will know how you can implement the relevant function with Git.

Why Not the Alternatives?

Git is a great toolbox, and many tasks can be solved using its various tools. In this section, we discuss alternative solutions and explain why we chose a tool.

There are both alternative strategies that do not make sense from our point of view or that do not work, as well as solutions that would work only in a different context. Here we will also discuss solutions that may be useful when it comes to special cases of the task.

This section explains more thoroughly our reasons for selecting the Git tool and shows you alternative solutions.

Chapter 14 Project Setup

Once you have decided to use Git, the first step would be to allocate files and directories for a Git repository. It is important to decide whether the project should be versioned in one repository or in multiple repositories. Since Git can only create a branch or a tag for the whole repository, the decision very much depends on the release units of your project.

After the project division is done, you must create a repository for each module and fill it. Empty directories and files that are not to be versioned will have special treatment.

When working in a team, for each module you must define a repository as the central repository. All developers will take advantage of this central repository to fetch the current status and record their changes.

You have to decide how all developers in the team can access the central repository. Git supports access via a shared network drive, through a web server, a proprietary network protocol and the Secure Shell Infrastructure (SSH).

Which protocol you choose depends on the existing infrastructure, local distribution, and the requirements relating to the administration of rights.

This workflow describes the following.

- how a project directory is converted into a repository,

- how empty directories are versioned,
- how to deal with the end of line problem
- which access options are available to a central repository and how this is set up, and
- how team members access the central repository.

Overview

This workflow is made up of two parts. In the first step, a repository for a project directory is created. In the second step, a central repository is made available to all developers.

Figure 14.1 shows how a project named **projecta** is transferred to a repository. Pay special attention to the empty directory named **EmptyDir**, because empty directories are not usually versioned by Git. You can force Git to version an empty directory by creating a file in it, such as **.gitignore**.

Likewise, during the initial commit you should make sure you do not version files that are not supposed to be in the repository, such as build results or temporary files. In the example you can see this in the **TempDir** directory. Backup files are stored in it even though this directory should not be versioned. To exclude this directory in future commits, you should create a **.gitignore** file in the root directory of the project and specify directories to be ignored in this file.

In the second step the new repository will be made available to other developers. In this case, Git supports different protocol variants:

- **file:** Access via a shared network drive
- **git:** Proprietary server service with network communication
- **http:** Access through a web server

- **ssh:** access via a secure shell infrastructure

In Git, multiple access points for the same repository can be deployed in parallel. For instance, it is common to configure a HTTP access for anonymous read access and an SSH access for write access.

Requirements

- **Shared server:** For collaboration with Git, one of the following must already exist: a shared network drive, a server computer that can start a service, a web server with CGI support or an SSH infrastructure.
- **Assignment of rights at the project level:** Git only recognizes reading and writing rights of the entire repository, i.e. it cannot assign fine-grain rights to individual directories.

Compact Workflow: Setting Up A Project

A project directory is imported into a new repository. This repository is provided as a central repository for the development team.

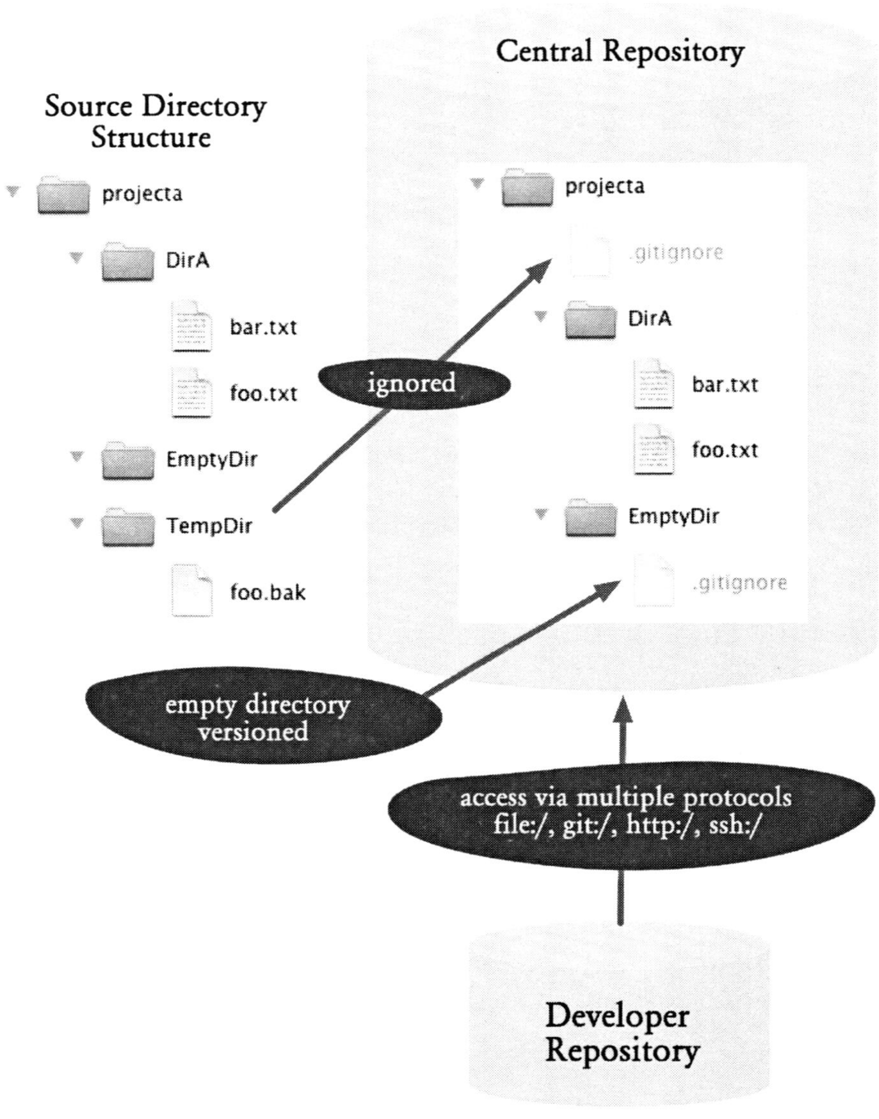

Figure 14.1: Workflow overview

Process and Implementation

The following procedures use the simple sample project **projecta** in Figure 14.1.

Create A New Repository from the Project Directory

This section shows how you can create a bare repository for an existing project. A bare repository is a precondition to share the repository with the team later.

The starting point is a directory in the file system that is gradually transformed into the finished bare repository.

Step 1: Prepare Empty Directories

Git is basically a content tracker, it can efficiently manage versions of files of different types. By contrast, directories are only considered structuring units and only versioned in conjunction with files.

Empty directories are not relevant in Git and cannot be added using the **add** command to a commit.

As long as the development environment is not dependent on the empty directories, you can just ignore them. Sometimes you cannot delete these empty directories because some development environments and tools assume the existence of these directories and they will complain if the empty directories are missing.

By adding a file to an empty directory, you can force Git to version the empty directory. Theoretically, you can add any file as long as it does not mean anything to the development environment. Adding a **.gitignore** or **.gitkeep** file should be okay.

As an example, you should do this to the **EmptyDir** directory in Figure 14.1. Using the Unix **touch** command, you can create an empty file in **EmptyDir**.

```
> cd projecta/EmptyDir
```

```
> touch .gitignore
```

Files whose names start with a dot are hidden files in Unix and ignored by many development environments.

Temporary files (such as build results) are often added to an empty directory. To prevent these files from being included by mistake in a commit, you can create a **.gitignore** file in the directory and insert a line with an asterisk ("*") to indicate to Git that all files in the directory must be ignored and should not show up as "untracked" when the **status** command is called.

The following Unix command **echo** creates a new **.gitignore** file and inserts "*" to it.

```
> echo "*" > .gitignore
```

Step 2: Ignore unnecessary files and directories

Development and build tools often create temporary files, such as class files in Java. These files should not be versioned. To prevent temporary files from being versioned, create a file named **.gitignore** and list all unwanted files and directories in it.

The **.gitignore** file can be created in each directory. The entries are always applied from this level and all its subdirectories.

The following is the content of a **.gitignore** file in the example in Figure 14.1. Each line specifies a pattern for a file name that should be ignored. In this case, the **TempDir** directory and all files with **.bak** extension should be ignored.

```
# Content of .gitignore
/TempDir
*.bak
```

To easily keep track of what files are ignored, create a **.gitignore** file only in the root of the project. Even deeper subdirectories can be excluded from that file. The only exceptions are the **.gitignore** files in empty directories where the files are only there to force Git to version the directories.

Step 3: Creating a repository

After the project files to be imported were prepared in the previous steps, in this step you create the repository.

```
> cd projecta

> git init
```

Step 4: Define treatment of line endings

Prior to actually importing files, you need to decide how to deal with line endings in text files.

Problems with line endings always occur when you develop simultaneously on different operating systems or when you use text files in different operating systems.

Windows uses CRLF (Carriage Return and Line Feed) to encode line breaks. Unix systems and Mac computers use LF (Line Feed) for line breaks. Text editors on different platforms deal with the line breaks of the other platforms, and, as such, this problem is largely solved.

However, a text editor, with or without the user's knowledge, adjusts the line breaks for the respective platform. This in turn means that Git recognizes a row as changed even though the content did not change. You can well imagine how many merge conflicts arise from it.

Git provides a solution to the problem by standardizing line breaks in the repository as LF. When the standardization is enabled, with every **commit** command Git converts all line endings to LF and slide in and out, if desired, in the respective platform-dependent default.

There are three different ways of dealing with line endings:

- **core.autocrlf false:** Line endings are ignored. Git stores line endings in the repository as they are present in the files. Also, when the files are retrieved, line endings remain unchanged.
- **core.autocrlf true:** Line endings are standardized (to LF) and changed to slide in and out for the respective platform.
- **core.autocrlf input:** Line endings are not adjusted when adding standardized (LF), but slide in and out.

Since you usually cannot prevent a repository from being used in the future on other platforms, it makes sense to work from the outset with standardized line breaks.

Therefore, on Windows systems, **core.autocrif** is set to **true** and on Unix systems it is set to **input** before the first import. Note that setting **core.autocrif** to **true** or **input** can be problematic if Git identifies a file as a text file where in fact it is a binary file. Use the **.gitattribute** file to override auto-detection.

Here is how to set **core-autocrlf** to **input**.

```
> git config --global core.autocrlf input
```

Step 5: Import files

Next, add all files for the first commit using the **add** command. All existing files, including the added **.gitignore** files, will then be committed and the ignored files left off.

Before you issue the **add** command, it is recommended to once again use the **status** command to check which files are reported as "untracked". Sometimes you forget a temporary file or directory by unintentionally adding it to the repository.

```
> git status
```

```
> git add .
```

A commit is concluded with the **commit** command.

```
> git commit -m "init"
```

Step 6: Create a bare repository

So far, we have created a normal repository with a workspace for the new project. To work in a team with a central repository using **pull** and **push** commands, the repository needs to be converted to a bare repository without a workspace. A bare repository consists only of the contents of the **.git** directory.

The conversion is done using the **clone** command and the **--bare** parameter. Bare repositories typically have the ending **.git**, to distinguish them from normal repositories.

```
> git clone --bare projecta projecta.git
```

The **--bare** option causes the clone to have no workspace and include only objects in the repository. The **projecta** parameter is the name of the repository to be prepared. The **projecta.git** parameter is the name of the bare repository to be created.

Sharing A Repository via File Access

This section describes how a bare repository can be shared using a shared network drive.

Step 1: Copy the bare repository

After a bare repository with the project files has been created, it can be easily stored on a network drive that is accessible to all.

```
> cp -R projecta.git /shared/gitrepos/.
```

In this example, we assume that the **/shared/gitrepos** directory is a network drive.

Step 2: Clone the central repository

When cloning a repository that has been shared over a network drive, simply specify the path to the central bare repository.

```
> git clone /shared/gitrepos/projecta.git
```

The path can be specified using the **file://** prefix.

```
> git clone file:///shared/gitrepos/projecta.git
```

Step 3: Manage the read and write access

The read and write access to the repository are managed through the file system. Each team member will have read access to the repository, because you need read permission to the bare repository directory. The same applies to the write permission.

Advantage and disadvantage

The advantage is the fact that in many corporate environments there are already shared network drives that are parts of a shared file system, the easiest option for a central repository.

The disadvantage is it is difficult to set up this option if you work in a different location than the central repository. Also, data access in Git is not the most efficient because remote Git commands (**push**, **fetch** and **pull**) must always work with remote data. In the following three server versions, however, Git can run remote commands on the server and only needs to transmit the result to the local machine.

Sharing A Repository Using the Git Daemon

The standard Git installation includes a built-in server service that provides access to the repository via a simple network protocol.

Note that the Git daemon in only available on Windows in Git version 1.7.4.

Step 1: Enable the bare repository for the Git daemon

When the Git daemon exports a repository, a **git-daemon-export-ok** file will be created in the root directory of the bare repository. The file can be empty and is only there to tell Git that it is okay to serve the project without authentication.

```
> cd projecta.git

> touch git-daemon-export-ok
```

Step 2: Start the git daemon

You start the Git daemon by using the **daemon** command.

```
> git daemon
```

Afterward, you can access all the repositories in the current computer that are approved for export. For this purpose, the full path to the repository must be specified in the Git URL.

Here is an example URL:

```
git://server-42/shared/gitrepos/projecta.git
```

The prefix **git:** indicates that the Git daemon must be used as the protocol. This is followed by the computer name (**server-42**) and the path to the directory (**/shared/gitrepos/projecta.git**) that is the location of the repository.

In order to make the URL not so dependent on a specific directory, it is often useful to specify a base path. This can be done using the **--base-path** parameter.

```
> git daemon --base-path=/shared/gitrepos
```

Now you can access the repository through **git://server-42/projecta.git**.

By default, the **daemon** command only exports a repository for reading. To enable write access to a repository, use the **--enable=receive-pack** parameter.

```
> git daemon --base-path=/shared/gitrepos --enable=receive-pack
```

The Git daemon can also be configured as a service in the operating system. For more details, see the documentation for the **daemon** command.

Step 3: Clone the central repository

When you clone a repository which is released via the daemon, just type in the URL to the central bare repository.

```
> git clone git://server-42/projecta.git
```

Step 4: Manage read and write access rights

The read and write access rights cannot be defined separately for individual developers in this variant. That is, each repository that was released for export can be read by anyone who has access to the computer.

If the Git daemon started with write access enabled, anyone can also change all the exported repositories.

Advantage and disadvantage

Advantage: The Git daemon provides the most efficient and fastest data transfer to and from the central repository.

Disadvantage: Lacking the capability to authenticate users, i.e., in environments where the read and write access rights must be limited to repositories, the Git daemon cannot be used.

Another disadvantage: In distributed teams, the firewall can still be a problem since the Git daemon requires a shared port.

Sharing A Repository via HTTP

The standard Git installation provides a CGI script that allows access to repositories through a web server. The CGI script is only available with Git version 1.6.6. Before that, it was possible to access a repository via HTTP, but the "old" protocol was very inefficient and slow.

As an example, the following describes the integration of the CGI script in an Apache2 infrastructure.

Apache2 is typically configured through a file called **httpd.conf**. The following describes what changes need to be made to the Apache2 configuration file. For details and background information, please read the Apache2 documentation.

Step 1: Enable Apache2 modules

CGI scripts can only be integrated with Apache2 if the **mod_cgi** module is enabled. In addition, for Git integration, you also need the **mod_alias** and the **mod_env** modules. You must enable these modules if they are not yet enabled.

Note that the exact paths in the following example depend on the Apache2 installation and the operating system.

```
LoadModule cgi_module libexec/apache2/mod_cgi.so
LoadModule alias_module libexec/apache2/mod_alias.so
LoadModule env_module libexec/apache2/mod_env.so
```

Step 2: Allow access to the CGI script

A typical Apache2 installation restricts access to the web server to certain directories in the file system. If you want to use the CGI script directly from the installation directory of Git, this directory needs to be enabled for access.

In this example, the CGI script is located in **/usr/local/git/libexec/git-core** directory. The following snippet will allow Apache2 to call the CGI script from there:

```
<Directory "/usr/local/git/libexec/git-core">
    AllowOverride None
    Options None
    Order allow,deny
    Allow from all
</Directory>
```

Attention! It is important to ensure that the user under which the server is running Apache2, has read and execute permissions over the CGI script.

Step 3: Allow access to the repository via HTTP

In order for the CGI script to export a repository, a file named **git-daemon-export-ok** must be created in the root directory of the bare repository. The file can be empty and is only there to tell Git that it is okay to serve the project without authentication.

```
> cd /shared/gitrepos/projecta.git

> touch git-daemon-export-ok
```

Attention! It is important to ensure that the Apache2 server has read and write access to the repository directory and all its files and subdirectories.

Now, you have to specify the root directory in the **httpd.conf** file, which contains the repositories to be exported. In this example it is the **/shared/gitrepos/** directory.

```
SetEnv GIT_PROJECT_ROOT /shared/gitrepos
```

Finally, you have to set up an alias for the CGI script. In this case it is **/git**.

```
ScriptAlias /git/ /usr/local/git/libexec/git-core/git-http-backend/
```

After you restart Apache2, access to all repositories under **/shared/gitrepos/** will be allowed.

Step 4: Clone the central repository

When you clone a repository, simply point the URL to the central repository. In this case, the URL consists of the machine name, the script alias for the CGI script, and the directory name of the repository.

```
> git clone http://server-42/git/projecta.git
```

In this example, the repository **projecta.git** is located on computer **server-42** under the alias script **git**.

Step 5: Manage read and write access rights

In this variant, the read and write permissions can be defined using the normal web server access rights.

For instance, to require a password when writing to the repositories (with the **push** command), add this entry in the Apache2 configuration file:

```
<LocationMatch "^/git/.*/git-receive-pack$">
    AuthType Basic
    AuthName "Git Access"
    AuthUserFile /shared/gitrepos/git-auth-file
    Require valid-user
</LocationMatch>
```

With this entry, all requests for **git-receive-pack**, which is required in every **push** command, will be intercepted and only allowed if the user is authenticated. Read access, on the other hand, are still possible without a password.

To protect both read and write access to a repository with a password, use this entry in the Apache2 configuration file.

```
<LocationMatch /git/projecta.git>
    AuthType Basic
    AuthName "Git Access"
    AuthUserFile /shared/gitrepos/git-auth-file
    Require valid-user
</LocationMatch>
```

More examples of the web server configuration can be found in the documentation for the **http-backend** command.

Advantage and disadvantage

Advantage: The HTTP variant allows easy access to repositories in a web environment. Typical problems with firewalls are not expected from the use of the HTTP protocol. Authentication can be done via the web server. If you need it to be more secure, you can use the HTTPS protocol.

Disadvantage: You need a web server, which must be operated and administered.

Sharing A Repository via SSH

In order to share a repository via Secure Shell (SSH), the necessary infrastructure must be in place. That is, you must at least have a computer with SSH daemon and all participants must have an SSH account on the server.

Step 1: Copy the bare repository

Simply copy the bare repository with the project files to an SSH host to which all developers have access. The **scp** command can be used to copy a file or files over SSH.

```
> scp -r projecta.git server-42:/shared/gitrepos/projecta.git
```

In this example, we assume that the computer (**server-42**) allows SSH access and that the **/shared/gitrepos** directory is allocated on this computer for storing the repository.

Step 2: Clone the central repository

When you clone a repository which is shared via SSH, you need a normal SSH path to the central repository.

```
> git clone ssh://server-42:/shared/gitrepos/projecta.git
```

The prefix **ssh://** can be omitted.

```
> git clone server-42:/shared/gitrepos/projecta.git
```

Step 3: Manage read and write access rights

In this variant, read and write access to the repository are managed by administering the SSH and file system rights. That is, each team member will have read access to the repository and need SSH access and read access to the repository directory. The same applies to the write permission.

Advantages and disadvantage

Advantages: Access to a repository over SSH is very easy to set up with an existing SSH infrastructure. Network access is very efficient, since most of the Git commands take place on the SSH server and only the results are transmitted over the network. Furthermore, the access is encrypted.

Disadvantage: If there is no existing SSH infrastructure, setting up this infrastructure can be costly. Even with the existing infrastructure, the management of user accounts can be complex, because each user needs a separate account, even for read access.

Note that you can use Gitolite (https://github.com/sitaramc/gitolite) and Gitosis (https://github.com/tv42/gitosis) software to simplify SSH infrastructure administration for Git. Gitolite can even manage read and write access rights at branch level. There is also Gerrit (http://code.google.com/p/gerrit/), which can also act as a SSH server in addition to providing review functionality.

Why Not the Alternatives?

Why Not Give up push?

The workflow described assumes that each developer has write access to the central repository and thus can publish their commits with the **push** command.

Typically, in an open source project, a pure pull sequence is used. In this case, all developers only work on their local repository and only the integration managers (integrators) have the permission to update the central software version.

Figure 14.2 shows this pure pull workflow.

The developers clone the central repository and generate new local commits. They then send the integrators a pull request, which is a request to import a branch or a commit and to merge it with the integration branch in the central repository.

The integrator is now responsible for merging all changes from all the developers to the central repository with the **pull** command. The integrator also takes the role of quality assurance. Once the integrator has all the changes in the central repository, the developers can import the official version from the central repository again with the **pull** command.

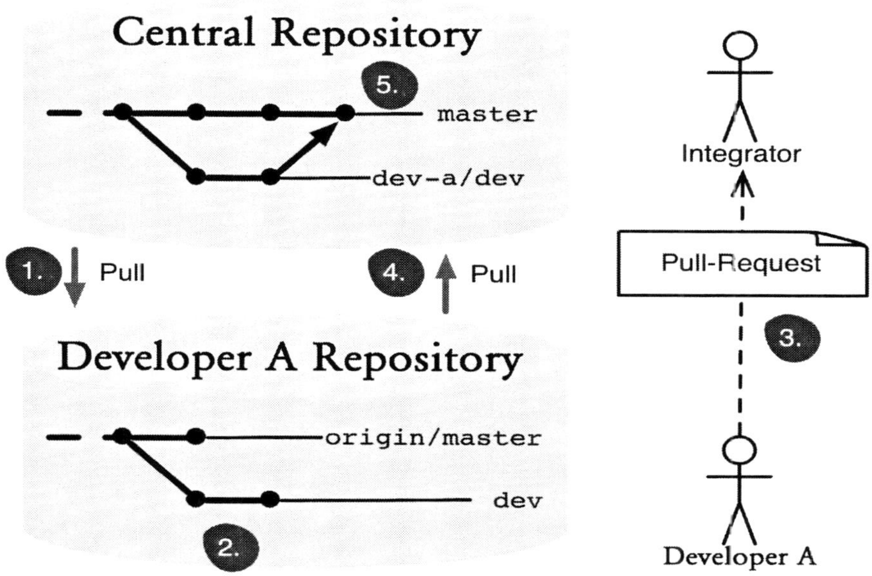

Figure 14.2: Working with pull only

In the normal project work and product development, this process can quickly become an unnecessary brake. There are always high-frequenters in a team who need to see the changes from the other parties quickly, such as when many files are changed in refactoring. The release cycles are shorter in agile projects. In such a scenario, the integrator can become a bottleneck and the changes are not built fast enough in the central repository.

In most projects, the advantage of having more control over changes in the official version does not weigh on the higher cost.

Another problem is the backup of changes. Only after the **pull** request has been processed, will data be stored in the central repository. Usually only the central repository is backed up by a backup system in enterprises. If the data is destroyed in the computer of the developer before the pull, work will be lost.

Note: It is of course also possible to back up the developer repository. In the open-source environment GitHub (https://github.com/) is often used for this purpose. This also ensures that the integrator can access the developer's repository.

Chapter 15 Developing on the Same Branch

In a centralized version control, such as Subversion, the team often works on a common branch. All developers copy this branch to their local workspace. There, changes take place, which are then written back to the version control system.

A very similar workflow can also be enacted with Git. This similarity facilitates transition and makes its use uncomplicated and fast.

Every developer creates a clone of the central repository and works on his or her copy of the **master** branch.

Once the development results are ready to be made available to others, the local **master** branch is merged with the central **master** branch. This results in merge commits, and at the same time changes are being made by other developers. The merge is done in the local repository, and the combined supernatant is then transferred to the central repository.

The advantage of this workflow is the rapid detection of conflicts, as changes from a developer are frequently pooled together with changes from other developers.

On the other hand, this workflow will create many merge commits, and as such clutter the commit history. It will no longer be possible to use the first-parent history used in the workflow "Working with feature branches."

The workflow in this chapter describes

- how local development on the **master** branch works,
- how one's own results are published in the central repository, and
- how the results may be used by other developers.

Overview

Figure 15-1 shows a typical scenario for this workflow. At the top is the central repository. At the bottom are Developer A's repository and Developer B's repository.

Every developer starts with his or her local **master** branch, producing small incremental commits necessary to return to a previous state and to document his or her steps.

Once a task is completed or if another developer needs the intermediate level, the commits are transmitted to the central repository with the **push** command. As long as the central master branch has not changed in the meantime, the **push** command will be successful.

However, often there will be commits from another developer on the central master branch. As such, the **pull** command must be used to merge the changes in the local repository with the changes from the central repository. This creates a merge commit in the local repository, which is then transmitted to the central repository with the **push** command. This is shown in Figure 15-1 as the last merge commit. Developer A had already transferred his commit, and Developer B had merges her commit with the existing commit.

A developer can also use the **pull** command to bring the changes from other developers into his or her own repository.

Requirements

- **The commit history does not have to be “nice”:** The commit history is only needed as a safety net against data loss and for comparison with the older versions. The workflow "Developing with feature branches” is another possible application of the commit history.
- **Continuous integration for the central master branch:** This workflow will create a lot of merge commits, so there is always a risk that there will be problems with the merged version. Therefore, it is important to continuously build the **master** branch on the central repository and perform testing so that the developers will learn of any problems that arise immediately.

Workflow: Developing on the Same Branch

All developers work on the same branch in their local repository and merge the results into the main branch on the central repository.

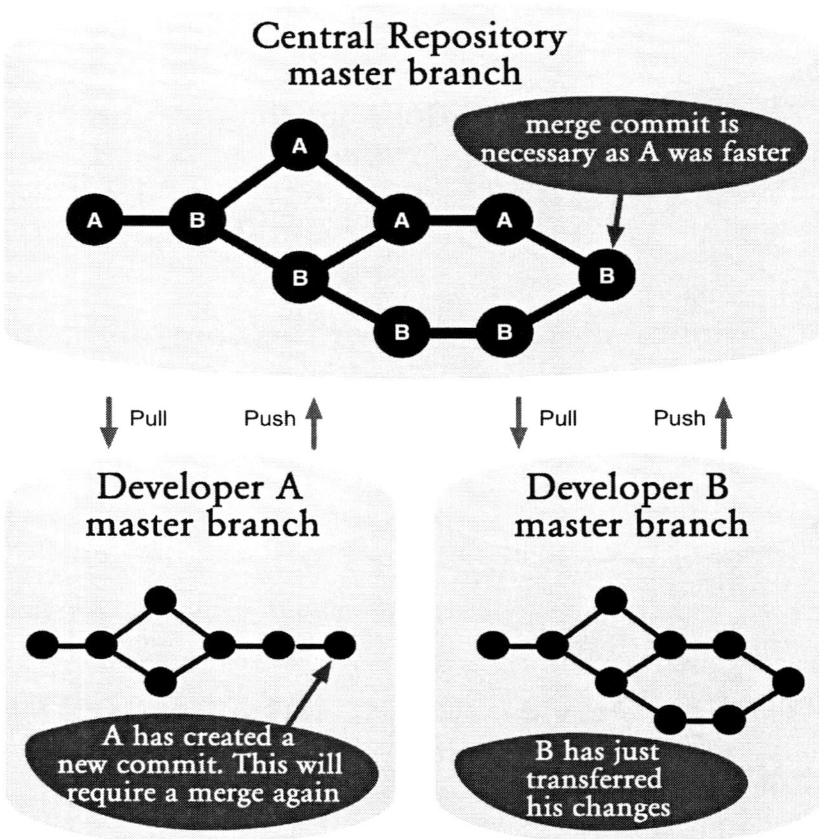

Figure 15.1: Workflow overview

Process and Implementation

For the following processes, we start from the central repository and a local clone of development.

Working on the master Branch

Step 1: Update the master branch

Before starting a new task, it is always advisable that you get the latest from the central repository. This way, the risk of file conflicts will be minimized.

If you want to make sure that there are no local commits that have not been transferred to the central repository, you should use the **--ff-only** parameter. This parameter prevents Git from automatically performing a merge with the central changes.

```
> git pull --ff-only
```

The **--ff-only** parameter prevents merge commits by allowing only fast-forward merges in the **pull** command.

Step 2: Make local changes

After pulling the current version of the **master** repository, development on the local machine can be carried out.

This will typically create incremental commits in Git, which include exactly a subtask, a unit of refactoring, or a fix. This way, the developers will be able to go back to a previous version or compare files with the current version. Before proceeding to the next step, this step should always be terminated with a commit of the local changes.

```
> git commit -m "Method X revised"
```

Step 3: Merge local changes with central changes

If the development tasks are completed or if another developer demands an intermediate version, the local changes must be transferred to the central repository.

Since this will only work if there were no changes in the central repository at that time, it is always advisable to move forward with the **pull** command to fetch all the central changes.

```
> git pull
```

```
 Already up-to-date.
```

If there were no changes when the **pull** command was executed, an "up-to-date" message will be printed.

If there were changes but Git was able to do a merge automatically, no "conflict" message will be displayed and Git will print the names of the files that had been changed.

```
remote: Counting objects: 5, done.
remote: Compressing objects: 100% (2/2), done.
remote: Total 3 (delta 0), reused 0 (delta 0)
Unpacking objects: 100% (3/3), done.
From projectX
   2cd173f..e10bb4d   master    -> origin/master
Merge made by recursive.
   foo |    1 +
   1 files changed, 1 insertions(+), 0 deletions(-)
```

If there are conflicts between the central and local changes, these will be displayed in the output.

```
remote: Counting objects: 8, done.
remote: Compressing objects: 100% (3/3), done.
remote: Total 5 (delta 0), reused 0 (delta 0)
Unpacking objects: 100% (5/5), done.
From projectX
   9139636..fa60160 master    -> origin/master
Auto-merging foo
```

CONFLICT (content): Merge conflict in foo Conflict resolution can be done in the normal way. The adjusted files of the previously incomplete merge commit are added using the **add** command. Subsequently, the conflicted merge needs to be completed using the **commit** command.

```
> git add foo
```

```
> git commit
```

If you do not provide a description for this **commit** command, Git will automatically generate a merge description that describes the conflicts that occurred.

```
Merge branch 'master' of projectX

Conflicts:
foo
```

Step 4: Transfer local changes to the central repository

If the previous step was successfully completed, there will be a consolidated project status in the local repository.

Before this version is transferred to the central repository, run the local tests to uncover any problems.

If you are satisfied with the quality of the version, you can transfer the local changes to the control center with the **push** command.

```
> git push
```

If the **push** command is terminated without an error message, that means the commits successfully arrived in the central repository.

If in the meantime another developer had done a commit, the **push** command will end with an error message:

```
To projectX.git
 ! [rejected]    master -> master (non-fast-forward)
error: failed to push some refs to '/Users/rene/temp/project.git/'
To prevent you from losing history, non-fast-forward updates were
rejected. Merge the remote changes (e.g. 'git pull') before pushing
again. See the 'Note about fast-forwards' section of
'git push --help' for details.
```

To get the new changes, you need to call the **pull** command again. Here, another merge commit will be created. In order not to complicate the history with two merge commits, you should delete the first merge commit with the **reset** command.

```
> git reset --hard ORIG_HEAD
```

The **--hard** parameter reconstructs both the workspace and the staging area in the specified commit. **ORIG_HEAD** in the command above is a symbolic name for the commit before the last **pull** or **merge** command.

Afterward, go back to Step 3 and bring the changes to the central repository with the **pull** command.

Why Not the Alternatives?

Why not **rebase** instead of **merge**?

The workflow described generates many merge commits, making the commit history difficult to read.

An alternative would be to merge the local changes with the central changes with a rebase (using the **--rebase** parameter with the **pull** command).

```
> git pull --rebase
```

With a rebase your local changes will be run again commit by commit on the central master branch. That is, a rebase will create new commits, but include the same changes.

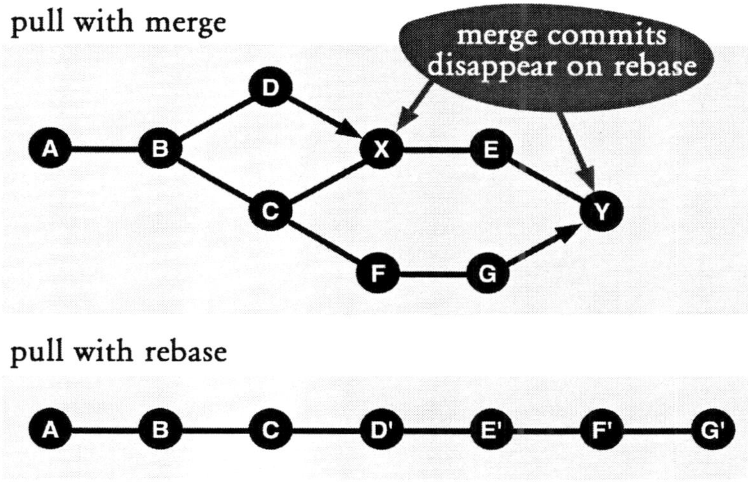

Figure 15.2: Rebase instead of merge

Figure 15.2 shows the different commit histories that will be generated with a merge and a rebase.

At first glance, it is striking to learn that there is no more branching in the rebase and thus the history is linear. This advantage is offset by the fact that its commits are now in the history, so a developer will never have detailed versions in his or her local environment. That always happens when multiple commits are copied using a rebase. As such, the developer can only review the last commit. In addition, the copied versions are not tested.

As an example, take commit **F'** in Figure 15.2. It is caused by a rebase of commit **G**. As long as there are no conflicts when copying the changes to commit **F**, this will be ignored. However, it is conceivable that there may have been substantive errors that cause this version to not work.

As long as you just want to know who has made what changes in the commits, you should be fine. However, once you try to troubleshoot in the commit history, those commits will start to be annoying.

If you will be working with rebase a lot, you can define the default behavior of the **pull** command by configuring the following setting:

```
> git config branch.master.rebase true
```

The **branch.master.rebase** parameter determines what branch rebase should be enabled by default. The branch name (**master**) can be replaced by any other branch name.

Chapter 16 Developing with Feature Branches

If everyone in the team is developing on the same branch, you will get a very confusing first-parent history with many merge commits. This will make it difficult to track changes for a specific feature or a bug fix. Especially for code review and troubleshooting, it is useful to know exactly which lines of code have been changed for a feature. Through the use of feature branches, Git can develop this information.

During feature development incremental commits are helpful at the time you need to fall back on an old functioning version. However, if you want to get an overview of the new features included in a release, coarse-grained commits make more sense. In this workflow, incremental commits on the feature branch and the release commits will be created on the **master** branch. The coarse-grained history of the **master** branch may well serve as the basis for the release documentation. The tester will welcome the coarse-grained commits with clear reference feature. This workflow shows how feature branches are used, so that

- commits that implement a feature are easy to locate,
- the first-parent history of the **master** branch includes only coarse-grained feature commits that can serve as release documentation,
- partial feature deliveries are possible, and
- important changes to the **master** branch during feature development can be used.

Overview

Figure 16.1 shows the basic structure that gets created when a team is working with feature branches. Starting from the **master** branch, a new branch is created for each feature or bug fix (bugs are not explicitly listed below). This branch is used to make all the changes and enhancements. Once the feature is ready to be integrated into the **master** branch, a merge is performed. Care must be taken to ensure that the merge is always initiated by the **master** branch and that fast-forward merges are not allowed. This produces a clear first-parent history on the **master** branch, which only includes merge commits of features.

If there are dependencies between features or if a feature is developed incrementally, then partial deliveries will be integrated into the **master** branch and then further developed on the feature branch.

Requirements

Feature-based approach: The planning of the project or product must be based on features, i.e. functional requirements are converted into feature work packages. There is a very small overlap between features.

Small features: The development of a feature must be completed in hours or days. The longer the development of the feature runs parallel to the rest of the development, the greater the risk that the integration of features incurs large expenses.

Local regression testing: Before the new feature is merged into the **master** branch , local regression tests need to be executed on the developer machine. It checks if the changes from the feature are compatible with the changes from other features and if there are unwanted side effects. If no such local regression tests are conducted, errors are often discovered only in the merged **master** branch. The correction of these errors would lead to a non-feature-based branch of history, and thus defeat the main advantage of feature branches.

Workflow "Developing with Feature Branches"

Each feature or bug fix is developed on a separate branch. After a feature or bug fix is completed, it is merged into the **master** branch.

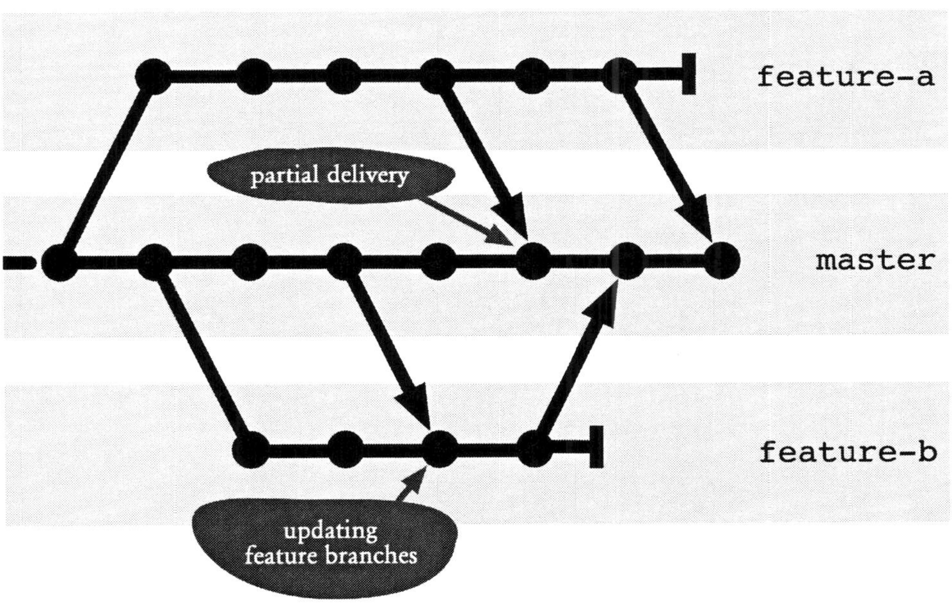

Figure 16.1: Workflow overview

Process and Implementation

The following operations assume the existence of a central repository. As usual, development takes place in a local clone. The central repository is accessed from the clone via the remote origin.

In the following flow, the **push** command is used to transmit local changes to the central repository.

When working with feature branches, you often have several branches in the local repository. Without a parameter, the **push** command only sends the currently active branch to the remote repository. You can change this behavior by setting the **push.default** option.

```
> git config push.default upstream
```

The default value matching would transfer all local branches for which there is the same remote branch. You would have to explicitly specify the branch at every **push** command to transfer only these.

Creating A Feature Branch

Once a new feature is ready to be processed, a new branch is created. It is important to ensure that the branch is always created starting from the **master** branch.

Step 1: Update the master branch

If there is access to the central repository, it makes sense to first bring the local **master** branch up to date. So that there may not be merge conflicts, do not work on feature-based tasks in the local repository on the **master** branch before you do this.

```
> git checkout master
```

```
> git pull --ff-only
```

The **--ff-only** parameter indicates that only fast-forward merges are allowed. In other words, if there are local changes, the merge will be canceled.

If the merge aborts with an error message, then you must have worked directly on the **master** branch by mistake. The changes need to first be moved to a feature branch.

Step 2: Creating a feature branch

The new branch can be created and work can begin.

```
> git checkout -b feature-a
```

It helps if the whole team agrees on consistent naming for feature and bug fix branches. Git also supports hierarchical names for branches, for example **feature/a**.

Often features and bug fixes are managed using a tracking tool (e.g. Bugzilla or Mantis). These tools assign unique numbers or tokens to features and bugs. These numbers can be used as branch names.

Step 3: Optional: Secure a central feature branch

Often, feature branches are created only locally, especially if they only have a short lifetime.

However, if a feature implementation takes longer or if more developers are working on the same feature, the intermediate results are particularly important. Then the branch can be secured in the central repository.

For this, you can create a branch in the central repository with the **push** command.

```
> git push --set-upstream origin feature-a
```

The **--set-upstream** parameter links the local feature branch with the new remote branch. That is, you can be spared from specifying a remote explicitly in all future **push** and **pull** commands.

The **origin** parameter specifies the name of the remote (the alias for the central repository) on which the feature branch is to be secured.

Future changes to the local feature branch can be guaranteed centrally with a simple **push** command call.

```
> git push
```

Integrating A Feature in the master Branch

As we have already defined in the requirements, it is important that features not exist long in parallel. Otherwise, the risk of merge conflicts and content incompatibilities increases greatly. Even if the feature will not be included in the next release, it is recommended that the integration be carried out promptly and the functionality be disabled with a feature switch.

This section describes how a feature is integrated with the **master** branch. It is important that the necessary merge be always executed in the **master** branch. Otherwise, no meaningful first-parent history can be obtained in the **master** branch.

Step 1: Update the master branch

Before the actual **merge** command, the local master branch has to be brought up to date. There will be no conflict if you do not work on the local **master** branch.

```
> git checkout master
```

```
> git pull --ff-only
```

Step 2: Merge the feature branch

The changes in the feature branch are transferred to the **master** branch with the **merge** command. So that the first-parent history of the **master** branch can serve as a feature history, fast-forward merges must not be allowed.

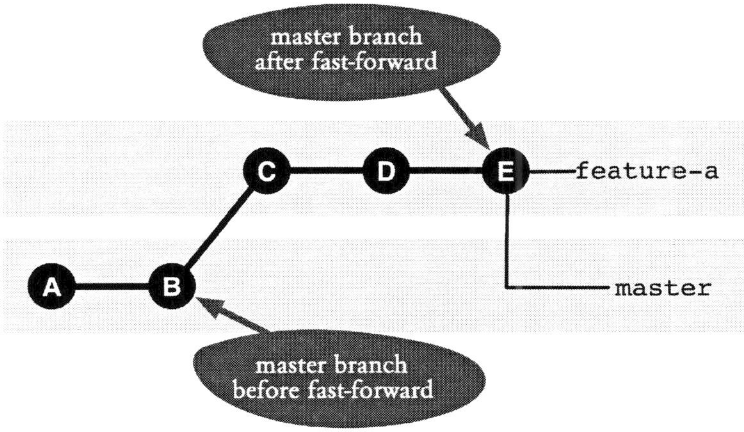

Figure 16.2: Problems with fast-forward and first-parent history

Figure 16.2 illustrates the problems that may occur with a fast-forward merge. Before the merge, the **master** branch points to commit **B** and the feature branch to commit **E**. After a fast-forward merge, the **master** branch is now also available on commit **E**. The first-parent history of the **master** branch would now include intermediate commits **D** and **C**.

The following command performs a merge and prevents a fast-forward merge:

```
> git merge feature-a --no-ff --no-commit
```

The **--no-ff** parameter prevents a fast-forward merge. The **--no-commit** parameter indicates that no commit should be carried out yet as the following tests might fail.

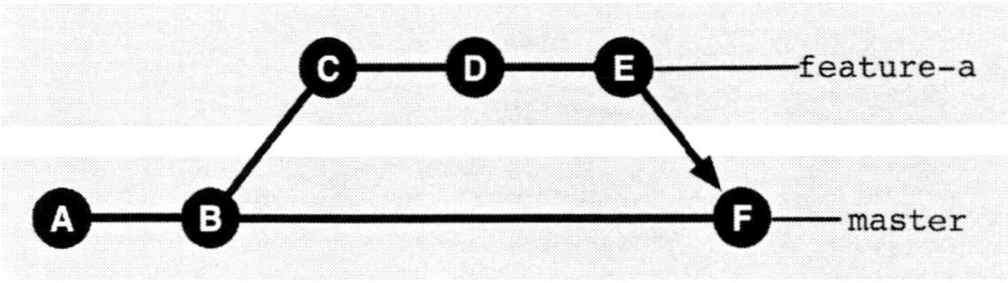

Figure 16.3: Merge without fast-forward

Figure 16.3 shows the commit history of the example if fast forwards are suppressed. The new merge commit **F** can be seen. The first-parent history of the **master** branch now does not include commits **C** to **E**.

This merge may cause conflicts if other features have changed the same files as those changed by the local feature. These conflicts must be resolved by the normal way.

Step 3: Do regression testing and create a commit

After the merge was performed, the regression tests need to be run. In this case, the tests check if the new feature caused errors in the other features.

If the tests result in errors, they must be analyzed. For troubleshooting, the currently performed merge must be discarded using the **reset** command.

```
> git reset --hard HEAD
```

The **--hard** parameter makes sure all changes in the staging area and workspace are discarded. **HEAD** indicates that the current branch must be the last closed commit.

Next, the feature branch is activated again. The errors will be rectified there and then this flow is repeated again starting from Step 1.

If the regression tests found no error, the commit can be completed.

```
> git commit -m "Delivering feature-a"
```

To use the **master** branch history as documentation, the comments in the merge commits should be set uniformly. In particular, it makes sense to accommodate the unique identification of the feature, such as the number. This makes it possible to search the features on the **master** branch later, using the **log** command and the **--grep** parameter.

Step 4: Transfer the master branch in the central repository

After the final step, the local repository will contain the reunification of the features with the **master** branch. In the next step the **master** branch must be transmitted to the central repository using the **push** command.

```
> git push
```

If errors occur for this command, another feature on the **master** branch must have already been integrated and a fast-forward merge is no longer possible. Normally you would now issue a **pull** command and merge the changes locally. In this case, however, the first-parent history would no longer be usable.

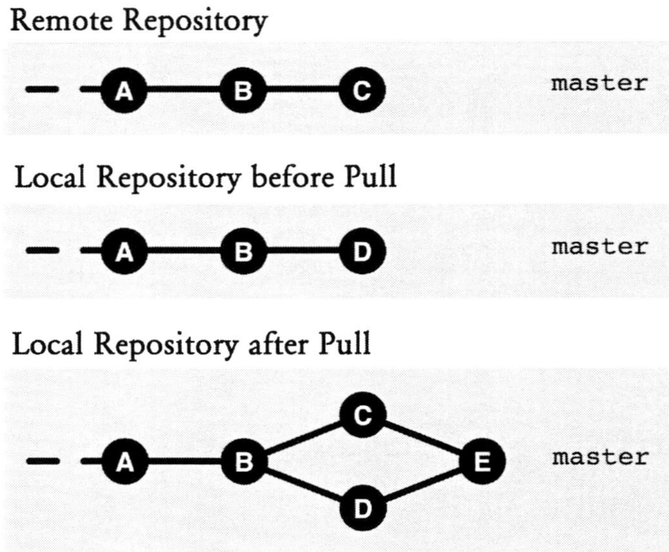

Figure 16.4 : No usable first-parent history after the pull command

The top and middle sections of Figure 16.4 outlines the situation described: Commit **C** would be the remote commit and **D** the locally applied commit. If you now issue a **pull** command, you would create a new merge commit **E** (bottom section of Figure 16.4). Thus, commit **C** would no longer be included in the first-parent history of the **master** branch.

In the first-parent history all the features should be included, so the local feature merge commit must be removed with the **reset** command in a failed **push** command.

```
> git reset --hard ORIG_HEAD
```

Here, **ORIG_HEAD** references the commit that was active before the merge in the current branch.

Subsequently, this sequence has to be started again from Step 1, i.e. the new commit must be retrieved with the **pull** command from the **master** branch.

If the **push** command was successful, the new feature is now included in the central repository.

Step 5: Delete or continue to use the feature branch Option

Variant 1: Delete the feature branch

If after merging with the **master** branch the feature development is complete, the feature branch can be deleted.

```
> git branch -d feature-a
```

The **-d** option deletes the given branch.

If deletion results in an error message, then chances are you forgot to merge the feature branch with the **master** branch. The **-d** option will only delete a branch if all commits in the branch are referenced by another branch. If you want to delete a feature branch without all its commits being taken over by the **master** branch, you can use the **-D** option. If the feature branch was secured in the central repository, the branch has to be deleted there as well.

```
> git push origin :feature-a
```

The colon before the branch name is important. The command means: Do not paste anything in the feature branch.

Variant 2: Resume feature development

If the feature development is not yet complete (i.e. the first integration with the **master** branch was only a partial delivery), the feature branch can be used further.

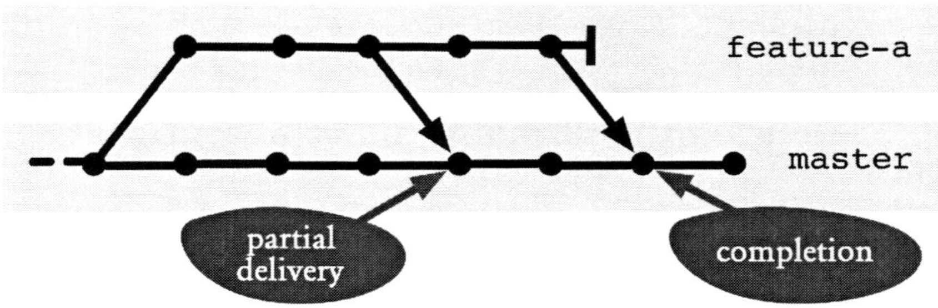

Figure 16.5: Resume work with a feature branch

In Figure 16.5, further work is outlined after a partial delivery. The branch continues to be used as the feature branch.

```
> git checkout feature-a
```

As soon as the next shipment is ready, normal integration with the **master** branch is performed again. In this case, Git is smart enough to take only the changes in the new commits in the **master** branch.

Transferring Changes on the Master Branch to the Feature Branch

In the best-case scenario, the development of a feature takes place independently of other features. However, sometimes there are important changes on the **master** branch that are necessary for the feature development, such as major refactoring or changes to basic services. In this case, the changes on the **master** branch need to be transferred to the feature branch.

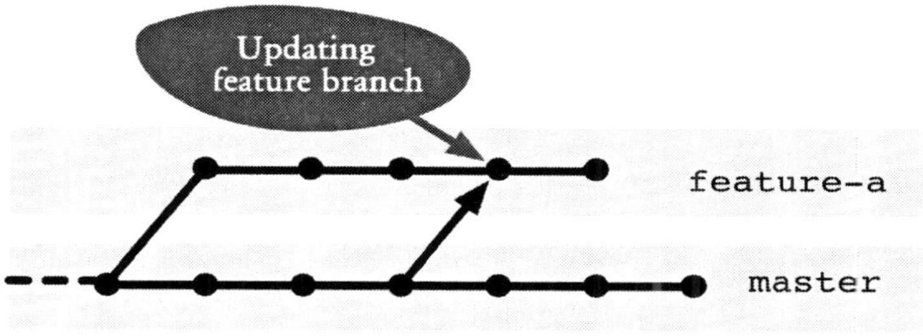

Figure 16.6: Changes on the master branch transferred to the feature branch

Figure 16.6 illustrates the situation. It is a merge from the **master** branch that needs to be performed on the feature branch.

Step 1: Update the master branch

First, the changes on the **master** branch must be imported to the local repository.

```
> git checkout master

> git pull --ff-only
```

The **--ff-only** option indicates that only fast-forward merges are permitted. This prevents you from accidentally performing a merge on the **master** branch.

Step 2: Apply changes in the feature branch

In the second step, the changes must be applied in the feature branch with a merge.

```
> git checkout feature-a

> git merge --no-ff master
```

Here, **--no-ff** prohibits fast-forward merges. A fast-forward merge can only happen at this point if the **master** branch and the feature branch have been merged right before this merge. A fast-forward merge would then destroy the first-parent history of the feature branch.

Any conflicts that arise must be resolved normally.

The feature branch can take any intermediate version from the **master** branch. Git can deal with multiple merges very well. However, the commit history would then be complex and difficult to read.

Git-Flow: High-Level OperationsGit Flow, which can be downloaded from https://githum.com/nvie/gitflow, is a collection of scripts that can be used to simplify the handling of branches, particularly feature branches. With this Git extension you can create and activate a new feature branch at the same time as follows:

```
> git flow feature start feature-a
```

Finally, the feature branch can be transferred to the **master** branch and simultaneously deleted.

```
> git flow feature finish feature-a
```

Why not the Alternatives?

Why not Continue to Work on the Merged Version after a Partial Delivery?

If a partial delivery of a feature occurs on the **master** branch, the **master** branch will contain a merge commit with changes of its own features and updates from other features. On the other hand, the updates from the other features are not yet available on the feature branch (See Figure 16.7).

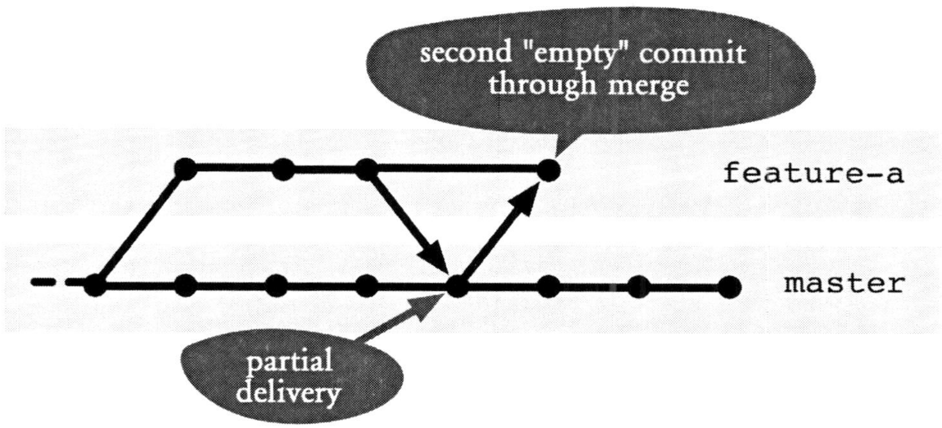

Figure 16.7: Another merge after a partial delivery

Wouldn't it make sense to perform a merge from the **master** branch into the feature branch and thus work on the merged branch?

The short answer is: The history would be unnecessarily complex, and in most cases, this procedure would bring no benefit to the feature development.

A merge of the **master** branch on the feature branch right after a partial delivery usually always leads to a fast-forward merge, i.e. both branches would point to the same commit. However, this would ruin the first-parent history of the feature branch—which changes were made in the course of the feature development would no longer be traceable. As such, you have to suppress the fast-forward merge, which in turn will lead to a new "empty" merge commit. That is, there would always be two merge commits for each partial delivery of a feature.

In most cases, it is not important for a feature development to be proceed on the most up-to-date version of the **master** branch.

If it is necessary to apply changes, then you can do that. However, it should not always be right after each partial delivery.

Why Feature Branches Are Not Integrated until Shortly before the Release?

When working with feature branches, release management often comes up with the idea, the decision, shortly before the delivery date, as to which features should be shipped with the new release.

Conceptually, it seems it is very easy to go with the feature branch approach too. Each feature is fully developed on a branch, but not yet integrated into the **master** branch. Which features will be integrated into the **master** branch are decided just before the D-day.

In an ideal world—where features are fully independent and no programming errors exist—this approach would work. In reality, however, this approach usually leads to major merge conflicts in integration and a long stabilization phase.

Furthermore, it is more complicated to develop features that have dependencies. Normally you would make a partial delivery of a feature on the **master** branch. In a solution with late integration of a feature, branches must exchange changes (see the following section). This would make independent integration of these features impossible to be carried out just before the release.

Also, proven processes for quality software, such as continuous integration with a build server, integration and refactoring are difficult to implement in late integration.

Why Not Exchange Commits between Feature Branches?

The workflow described provides no direct exchange of commits between feature branches. The integration always takes place on partial deliveries on the **master** branch.

Wouldn't it be easier to perform a merge directly between feature branches?

Step by Step
ReReRe – Automatic conflict resolution

Manual conflict resolution in files can be recorded. If the same conflict occurs again and again, the resolution can be applied automatically. This is called "Reuse recorded resolution." In short: ReReRe.

1. Enable ReReRe
The feature to record conflict resolutions must be enabled once for each repository.

```
> git config rerere.enabled 1
```

Rerere stores conflict resolutions locally, as such ReReRe must be enabled in every clone.

2. Record conflict resolution
Once ReReRe is enabled, all conflict resolutions conducted will be saved automatically to files with every **commit** command. However, if no commit is performed (e.g., if the attempt is rejected with a **reset** command), the **rerere** command must be invoked explicitly:

```
> git rerere

Recorded resolution for 'foo.txt'.
```

3. Apply conflict resolution
Once ReReRe is enabled, Git will attempt to resolve conflicts automatically at every merge attempt. Here, although the files are changed in already solved conflicts, no **add** command is called to confirm the conflict resolution.

```
> git merge featureE

Auto-merging foo.txt
CONFLICT (content): Merge conflict in foo.txt
Resolved 'foo.txt' using previous resolution.
Automatic merge failed; fix conflicts and then commit the
result.
```

After you take over control to resolve the conflicts, you must add the affected file to the next commit using the **add** command.

```
> git add foo.txt
```

Step by Step
Showing open feature branches

We need to show feature branches that have not been merged with the master branch.

1. Show open feature branches
If you work consistently with feature branches, you often have more than one active feature branch in your repository. The **branch** command can display all branches that have not been merged.

```
> git branch --no-merged master
```

The **--no-merged** option shows all branches with commits that have not been included in the **master** branch, i.e. all the feature branches that have not yet been merged with the **master** branch.

The decisive advantage of feature branches is the simple and comprehensible history. Add merges directly between feature branches, and this advantage goes away.

Step by Step
Show all changes in a merged feature

All changes of a feature should be shown as a diff.

It is important to find out which changes were made. This is especially true when doing a code review. Figure 16.8 is an example of a feature branch with a partial delivery and a final delivery. Subsequently, the commits are referenced according to this figure.

1. Locate the commits of a feature

For a diff you need all the commits of the feature in the **master** branch. Normally, there will only be one merge commit, except when partial deliveries were made: Then there will be several commits. In the example, commits **H** and **G** are found.

```
> git checkout master

> git log --first-parent --oneline --grep="featureC"

c52ce0a Delivery featureC
c3a00bc PartialDelivery featureC
```

The **--grep** option searches the log for the given piece text.

2. Do a diff

The changes can be viewed by doing a **diff** between the commits found and with their respective first parent. In the example, the changes between commit **B** and commit **G** and between commit **G** and commit **H** are shown.

```
> git diff c3a00bc^1 c3a00bc
> git diff c52ce0a^1 c52ce0a
```

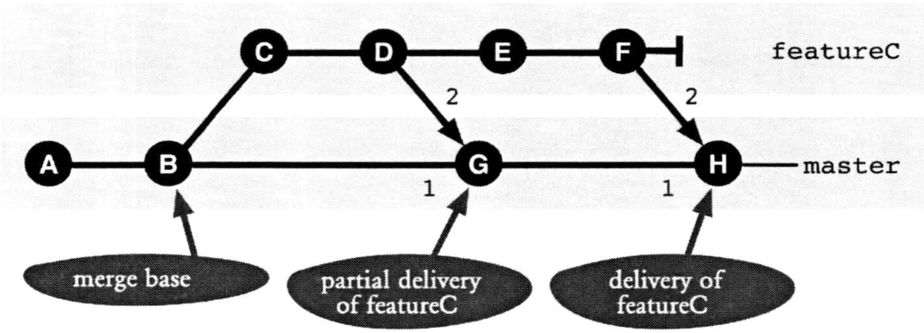

Figure 16.8: An example of a feature branch

Step by Step
Finding all commits of a feature branch

All commits that were created during feature development, will be displayed.

During a code review you want to understand more thoroughly how changes in a feature branch were built in. It may be useful to look at all the commits of the feature branch individually. Figure 16.8 is an example of a feature branch with a partial delivery and a final delivery. Subsequently, the commits are referenced according to this figure.

1. Find merge commits of the feature

First, you need all the commits on the **master** branch that have something to do with the feature. Normally, there will only be one merge commit, except where there are partial deliveries, in which case there will be several commits. In the example commits **H** and **G** are found.

```
> git checkout master

> git log --first-parent --oneline -grep="featureC"

c52ce0a Delivery featureC
c3a00bc PartialDelivery featureC
```

The **--grep** option searches the log for the given piece of text.

2. Find the start of the feature branch
To display all commits, you need to find the commit on the **master** branch from which the feature branch branches. The starting point is the lowest commit, which was found in the previous step (commit **G**). This must be a merge commit with two parents. You can find the commit with the **merge-base** command. This commit is the common starting point of the first parent (commit **B**) and the second parent (commit **D**), the merge base (commit **B**).

```
> git merge-base c3a00bc^2 c3a00bc^1

ca52c7f9bfd010abd739ca99e4201f56be1cfb42
```

3. Show feature commits
Once the starting point has been found, you can display all commits of the feature branch with the **log** command. To do this, ask what commits are necessary for the merge base (commit **B**) to be the last commit of the feature branch. The last commit of the feature branch is the second parent (commit **F**) of the last delivery (commit **H**).

```
> git log --oneline ca52c7f..c52ce0a^2
```

Chapter 17 Troubleshooting with Bisection

During development, it often happens that an error that was not present in earlier versions suddenly appears in functionality that has already been successfully tested. A promising strategy for debugging is to search for the commit in which the error can be observed for the first time. Since when working with Git you typically produce small commits, you can analyze the changes and find the cause quickly.

Git supports searching for faulty commits with bisection.

Bisection is based on a binary search. Starting from a known good commit and a known faulty commit, this commit history is "halved" and the "middle" commit is activated in the workspace. The active commit can then be examined for the error. Depending on whether or not the error is found in the active commit, the remaining of the history in which the error must be hiding is again "halved" and a new "middle" commit is selected. In the end, you will normally find the commit in which the error first appears.

This workflow shows

- how to use bisection to find faulty commits efficiently, and
- how to automate troubleshooting with bisection.

Overview

Figure 17.1 shows a commit history with a commit that is error free and another commit that is known to be faulty. A commit history does not need to be linear. However, there must be a path from the faulty commit to the error-free commit through parent relationships between the two commits.

When a bisection process is started, Git selects a suitable commit in the middle of the history. This commit can then be tested either manually or with a script and marked as "good" or "bad." Next, the bisection task picks another commit and examines and marks it. This process is repeated until it finds a commit with the error whose direct predecessor is error-free.

Requirements

Reproducible error detection: The fault must be proven consistent, i.e., it is possible clearly to identify one version as correct or incorrect. An automated error detection, using a test case or script, must be able to detect the error.

The error detection must not be expensive: The error detection must be fast and not costly. With bisection multiple fault detections are required depending on the number of commits examined. If the time required or the cost is too great, an analytic search for the cause of the error will be more efficient.

Workflow "Troubleshooting with bisection"

During development, an error occurs, which was not present in previous versions. Bisection locates the commit that has introduced the error in the commit history.

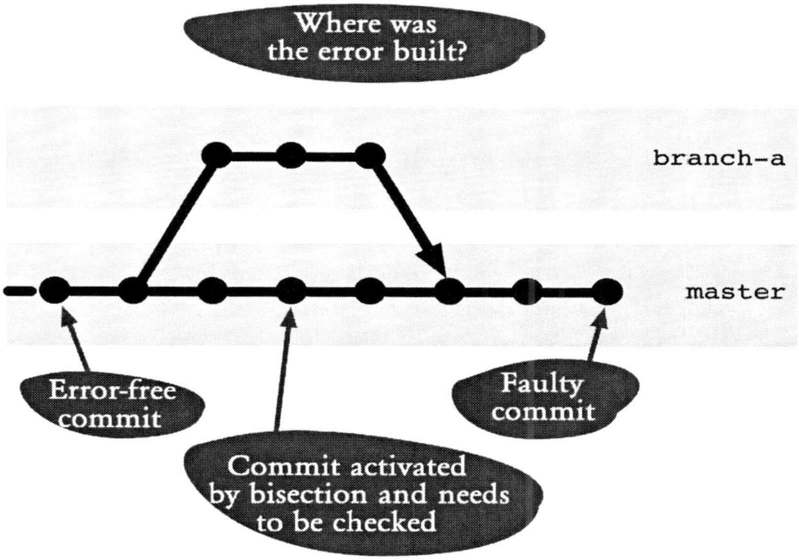

Figure 17.1: Workflow overview

Process and Implementation

For the following operations, we have a small sample project that implements various mathematical functions. Among other things, it calculates the factorial of a number and returns a list of all factorials of 1 to 5.

```
> java FactorialMain
```

```
Factorial of 1 = 1
Factorial of 2 = 1
Factorial of 3 = 2
Factorial of 4 = 6
Factorial of 5 = 24
```

Manual Troubleshooting with Bisection

The first process describes the basic procedure of bisection, in which the test is carried out manually because of an error.

Step 1: Define the error indicator

Typically, an error will be caught by a developer, tester or user.

The first step is to analytically understand the error situation and find an indicator of the error.

The following points are examples of error indicators:

- An action or a function call raises an exception, the program is canceled or an error message is displayed.
- A function returns an erroneous result for certain entries.
- A test case fails.

In our example, the factorial of 3 can be seen as an indicator that there is an error.

In many cases, this analysis alone already leads to finding the cause and bisection is no longer necessary.

Step 2: Find the error-free and faulty commit s

The bisection process requires an error-free commit and an erroneous commit. A good candidate for a flawless commit is the last release or the last milestone.

If you find out that the potential candidate for an error-free commit also contains the error, you should go further back in history.

Finding an erroneous commit should not be hard because the error was already reported. However, if more flawed commits are found when searching for flawless commits, it makes sense to select the oldest known erroneous commit.

Below is the log output from our example that shows the commit history.

```
> git log --oneline

202d25d modulo finished
e36fead multiply finished
918ed2f sub finished
ebe741d add finished
87ac59e ComputeFactorial finished
39cbdc0 init
```

Analysis shows that commit **87ac59e ComputerFactorial finished** is error free and commit **202d25d modulo finished** is incorrect.

Step 3: Troubleshoot with bisection

Now that the error has been confined to an area in the commit history, the actual search for the error can start with bisection.

You start bisection with the **bisect start** command. You must specify the faulty commit as the first parameter and the error-free commit as the second parameter.

```
> git bisect start 202d25d 87ac59e

Bisecting: 1 revision left to test after this (roughly 1 step)
[918ed2f29a44e468d690fb770aab1ad2dbae1a5a] sub finished
```

The **bisect start** command marks the first commit as the bad commit and the second commit as the good one. Subsequently, the commit located between the two commits (in this case, commit **918ed2f sub finished**) is activated.

Now the workspace contains files from a commit that we are not yet sure is faulty or faultless. Thanks to the error indicator found, the version status can now be tested.

```
> java FactorialMain
```

```
Factorial of 1 = 1
Factorial of 2 = 1
Factorial of 3 = 2
Factorial of 4 = 6
Factorial of 5 = 24
```

The result from running **FactorialMain** in the workspace shows that the error is still there, which means the current commit is faulty.

We can now mark the current commit with one of the following commands.

- **bisect good:** The error was not observed; the commit is error-free.
- **bisect bad:** The error was observed; the commit is faulty.
- **bisect skip:** The current commit cannot be tested. Typically, it is because it does not compile or missing files. Bisection will activate another commit to test.

In our example, the error is still present and we mark the commit as "bad."

```
> git bisect bad
```

```
Bisecting: 0 revisions left to test after this (roughly 0 steps)
[ebe741de3366a3fc08fbedfdfa408517dd172ca3] add finished
```

In response Git reports that now commit **ebe741d add finished** is activated. In addition, Git reports that this is the last commit that must be tested.

The re-testing of our **FactorialComputer** shows that this commit is error-free, and the commit will be marked as "good."

```
> git bisect good
```

```
commit 918ed2f29a44e468d690fb770aab1ad2dbae1a5a
Author: Rene Preissel <rp@eToSquare.de>
Date:   Fri Jun 24 08:04:43 2011 +0200

    sub finished

:040000 040000 0e5bfb07e859072a564eaca073461e4a12a0ed61 \
329e7f864bac874c69be4531452c753cf56be794 M     src
```

Git now tells us that the commit **918ed2f sub finished** is the first commit where the error occurs. Now you can analyze the changes in the commit using Git commands (for example, **git show 918ed2f**).

Finally, it was found in our example that the factorial was calculated only up to *n*-1.

Note that before troubleshooting begins, the workspace must be set to the HEAD of the current branch again. This will be described in the next step.

Step 4: Stop or cancel bisection

After a successful root cause analysis with bisection or after deciding a bisection operation should be canceled, the workspace must be reset to the normal version of development with the **bisect reset** command .

```
> git bisect reset

Previous HEAD position was ebe741d... add finished
Switched to branch 'master'
```

Automated Troubleshooting with Bisection

In the previous sequence, the test was to determine whether or not a commit contains a bug and was carried out manually. If the confined area of the history is very long or the test is manually very expensive, then you can also automate the test with a script and let bisection do its job.

Step 1: Define the error indicator

The error indicator is defined the same way as the manual troubleshooting with bisection. It is only necessary to ensure that the indicator can be checked automatically with a script.

Step 2: Prepare a test script

To automate troubleshooting with bisection, you have to provide a shell script that can detect the error indicator automatically. The shell script must return a different exit code depending whether or not the error is present.

- **Exit code 0:** The error was not found. Bisection should mark the commit as "good."
- **Exit codes 1-124**, **126**, **127**: The error was found. Bisection should mark the commit as "bad."
- **Exit code 125:** The test could not be performed because the application does not work. Typically, this version is not compilable. Bisection should skip the commit.

Our calculator application was written in Java. As an example, we show how debugging can be automated using bisection in this environment. In other development environments, the individual scripts need to be adjusted accordingly.

Automatic verification of the actual fault is performed by a JUnit test (JUnit can be downloaded from http://www.junit.org). It simply checks if the factorial of 3 is really 6. If the result is false, then the test will fail.

```
public class FactorialBisectTest {
    @Test
    public void testFactorial() {
        long result = Computer.factorial(3);
        Assert.assertEquals(6, result);
    }
}
```

Warning. It is important to implement this test in a new file. This file should not be versioned in Git. In a bisection process different commits are activated in the workspace one after the other. If the test file is under Git control, this file would no longer be present when an old commit is activated. On the other hand, non-versioned files will leave the change in the workspace.

The automated bisection process requires a shell script. This shell script must first compile our Java source files and then start the test.Ant is used as the build system in our example. In the Computer project, there is a build file named **build.xml** that can perform a clean build (**ant clean compile**). To run the bisection testing, another build file, named **bisect-build.xml**, is also provided that contains only one target to start the test. Note that this file should not be versioned with Git.

```
<target name="test">
    <junit>
        <classpath refid="build.classpath" />
        <test name="FakultaetsBisectTest"
                haltonerror="true"
                haltonfailure="true"/>
    </junit>
</target>
```

To access the various Ant targets, there is a shell script called **bisect-test.sh**. This script is also not versioned with Git.

```
#!/bin/bash

ant clean compile
if [ $? -ne 0 ];then
    exit 125;
fi

ant -f bisect-build.xml
if [ $? -ne 0 ];then
    exit 1;
else
    exit 0;
```

```
fi
```

This script calls the various build targets on and checks the exit code of Ant. On failure Ant returns an exit code other than 0. This needs to be converted to the desired code from the bisection process.

- If the build fails, then exit code 125 is returned.
- If the test is successful, exit code 0 is returned.
- If the test fails, the exit code of 1 is returned.

Step 3: Find an error-free and a defective commits

The search for a fault-free and a faulty commits is no different from the manual process. However, you can also use the JUnit test to check for the error. As an example, we select commit **87ac59e FactorialCompute finished** and verify that it is error-free.

```
> git checkout 87ac59e

> ant -f bisect-build.xml

Buildfile: bisect-build.xml

test:

BUILD SUCCESSFUL
Total time: 0 seconds
```

Warning. After the process, do not forget to set the **master** branch back as the active branch.

```
> git checkout master
```

Step 4: Automated troubleshooting with bisection

With automated troubleshooting, bisection is also started with the **bisect start** command as the first bisection process. Also, the faulty commit is passed as the first parameter and the error-free commit as the second parameter.

```
> git bisect start 202d25d 87ac59e
```

```
Bisecting: 1 revision left to test after this (Roughly 1 step)
[918ed2f29a44e468d690fb770aab1ad2dbae1a5a] sub finished
```

Then the **bisect run** command is used to execute the **bisect-test.sh** shell script.

```
> git bisect run ./bisect-test.sh
```

The following output is truncated, showing only the last lines of the **bisect run** command. It is good to see that the command finds **918ed2f sub finished** as the first erroneous commit.

```
 ..
Buildfile: bisect-build.xml

test:

BUILD SUCCESSFUL
Total time: 0 seconds
918ed2f29a44e468d690fb770aab1ad2dbae1a5a is the first bad commit
commit 918ed2f29a44e468d690fb770aab1ad2dbae1a5a
Author: Rene Preissel <rp@eToSquare.de>
Date:   Fri Jun 24 08:04:43 2011 +0200

    sub finished

:040000 040000 0e5bfb07e859072a564eaca073461e4a12a0ed61 \
 329e7f864bac874c69be4531452c753cf56be794 M    src
bisect run success
```

Step 5: Complete the bisection operation

After the successful troubleshooting, the bisection process must end the procedure with a **bisect reset** command.

```
> git bisect reset

Previous HEAD position was ebe741d... add finished
Switched to branch 'master'
```

Why Not the Alternatives?

Why Not Use merge to Add the Test Scripts in Old Commits?

The procedure described takes advantage of the fact that Git leaves unversioned files in the workspace when a new commit is activated. This makes it possible to execute the "new" test scripts in old commits.

An alternative solution will be to incorporate the test scripts into a new branch (see the **bisect-test** branch in Figure 17.2).

In the bisection shell script, a merge of the **bisect-test** branch with the commit currently selected by bisection is now performed before each test run. The option **--no-commit** is used to prevent a permanent commit.

After the test has been performed, the changes resulting from the merge are reset using the **reset** command.

This sequence and an example script can be found in the online documentation of the **bisect** command in the Example section.

The solution that uses the **bisect-test** branch can be useful not only when a test case and new test scripts have been added. It can also be useful when existing code for the test must be adapted, for example because a review needs to access data not visible in the old commits.

However, the process that uses unversioned files that we described is sufficient and easier to implement in most cases.

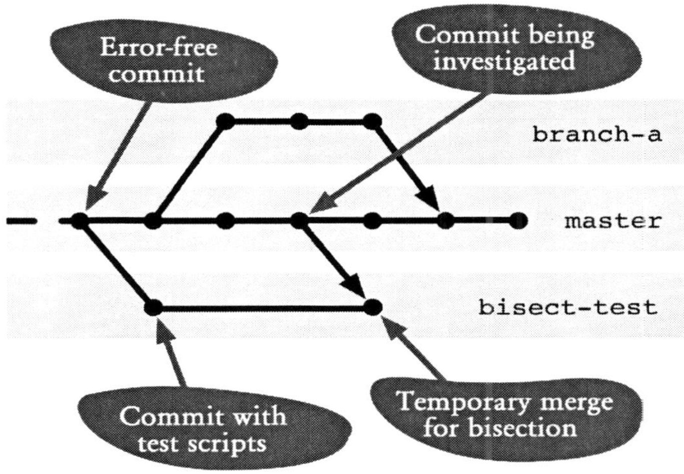

Figure 17.2: Using the bisect-test branch

Chapter 18 Working with A Build Server

Many projects use a build server such as Hudson, Jenkin or Cruise Control to carry out regular automated builds with unit tests and integration tests. Git can naturally serve as a source for software to be built. It is interesting when information about successful builds also flow into the Git repository. If a repository knows which version was last successfully built and tested, the developer can see with a simple **diff** command how its local development differs from this version. Moreover, it will be possible to construct a branch with a history of successfully tested versions. This is very useful if you later want to fix a tricky error that was not caught by the tests.

This workflow shows how to integrate Git such that

- the current version will be built and tested regularly,
- the developer at any time will be able to compare their workspace with the last successfully tested version, and
- a history will be built on successfully tested versions to assist in troubleshooting.

Overview

The brain of this workflow is the build server (see Figure 18.1). The build server is configured such that it brings the latest commits from the **master** branch of the central repository in the build repository regularly. In the build server, the sources are built and tested.

There will be two branches in the build repository. The **last-build** branch simply refers to the version in the **master** branch that was last built successfully. The **build-history** branch contains all successfully built versions of the software.

The **last-build** branch is transferred to the build server after each successful build in the central repository. With a **diff** command against the **last-build** branch, every developer can always show which changes have not yet been tested successfully.

In the event of a hard to find error, the developer can get the **build-history** branch from the build server to his/her local repository and check in which successfully built version the error first appeared.

Requirements

Central repository: The project uses a central repository that defines the current status of the software.

Continuous integration: The development for the next release is regularly integrated into a common branch (the **master** branch). This integration will not happen only at the end of development, but immediately after a change is completed.

Build server: The project uses a build server to do automated builds and tests.

Test suite: There must be a suite of unit tests and or integration tests that can be started with a script.

Workflow "Working with A Build Server"

A build server builds and test the current version of the software regularly. As a result, we get a history of successfully built versions. In addition, the last successful build is marked in the central repository.

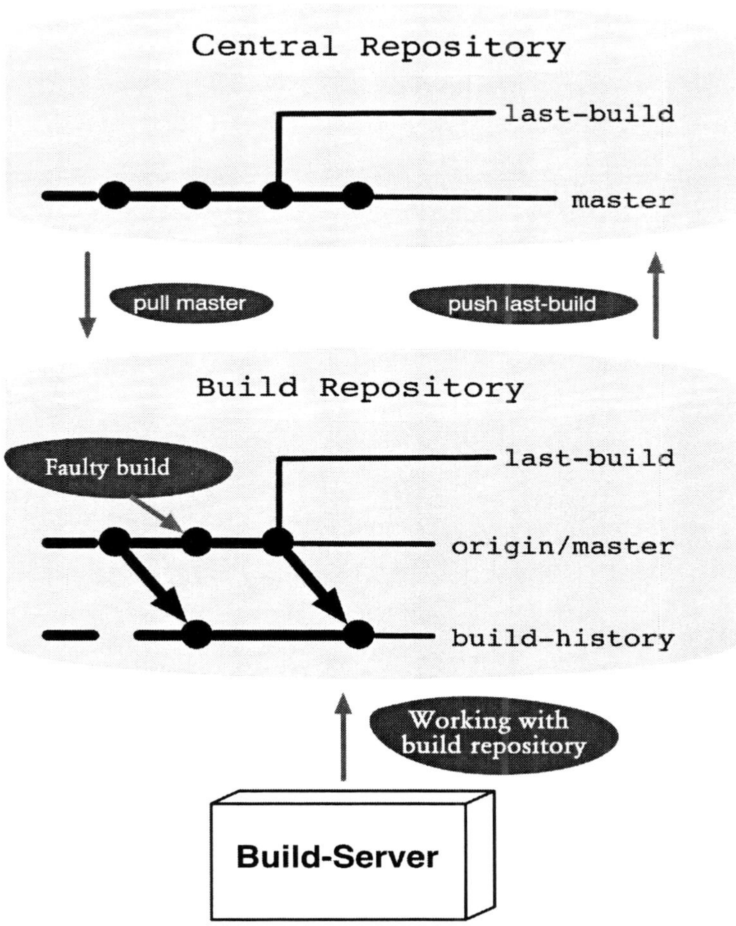

Figure 18.1: Workflow overview

Process and Implementation

Preparing the build server

A separate repository must be set up for the build server. The easiest way to create a build repository is by using the well known **clone** command. Using **clone**, however, would clone the entire central repository with all the branches. As a matter of fact, for the build server we only need the **master** branch and perform an **init** and a **fetch** commands on it.

Step 1: Create an empty build repository

First, create a new empty repository.

```
> mkdir buildrepo

> cd buildrepo

> git init
```

Step 2: Get the master branch from the central repository

With the **remote add** command we link the build repository with the central repository. To prevent fetching all the branches with the **fetch** or **pull** command, we specify a branch explicitly with the **-t** parameter.

```
> git remote add -t master origin <central repo>
```

The parameters used in the command are

-t master: Only the **master** branch is automatically transferred at a future **fetch**, **pull** and **push** command.
origin: The name of the newly added remote. We chose the same remote name on purpose so that the clone command would also use this name.
<centrl repo>: The URL to the central repository.

So far, no commits have been transferred from the central repository to the build repository. So, first we will do a **fetch** to transfer the data.

```
> git fetch
```

Step 3: Create a build-history branch

As the last step, we need to create a new branch called **build-history** that will contain a history of successful builds. It is recommended that the branch start at the first commit of the **origin/master** branch.

If we were to start the **build-history** branch at the current commit of the **origin/master** branch, existing commits on the **origin/master** branch would be included in the build history.

Unfortunately, there is no simple Git command to find the first commit of a branch. The best thing we can do is output the log and look for the last entry.

```
> git log --cneline --first-parent origin/master| tail -1

3a05e26 init
```

The parameters used in the command are as follows.

--oneline: Prints only one line of the commit log.

--first-parent: Prints only the first parents of the commits. This will lead to less processing and thus a faster result.

origin/master: The first commit should come from the master branch on the central repository.

| tail -1: Prints only the last line of the log output.

After the first commit is found, the **build-history** branch can be created and activated. We can also specify the start commit with the **checkout** command.

```
> git checkout -b build-history 3a05e26
```

The **-b** option creates a new branch and activates it in the workspace.

Git on the Build Server

The following steps describe how to work with Git on the build server. Typically they would be implemented in a script and integrated into the respective build server infrastructure.

The build server always works on the **build-history** branch.

Step 1: Get the changes from the central repository

The latest commits are fetched from the **master** branch on the central repository.

```
> git fetch
```

Step 2: Check if a build is required

You need to check if there are fresh commits by comparing the current **build-history** branch with the **origin/master** branch using the **diff** command. If no difference is detected, the build must not even be started and the process should be terminated.

```
> git diff --shortstat --exit-code origin/master
1 files changed, 68 insertions(+), 144 deletions(-)
```

The parameters used in the command are

- **--shortstat:** With this option, not all changes will be displayed in detail. Instead, only a brief statistics on the number of changed files will be displayed.
- **--exit-code:** This option ensures that the command returns 1 if there are differences (otherwise 0). This way, you can evaluate the result easily.
- **origin/master:** The difference is to be checked against the **master** branch on the central repository.

Step 3: Clean up the workspace

If a previous build has failed, the local workspace will contain the merge results of this broken build. You should reset the workspace just to be safe.

```
> git reset --hard HEAD
```

You can delete all unversioned files with the **clean** command.

```
> git clean --force
```

The **--force** option forces the execution of the clean command.

Step 4: Bring changes to the local build-history branch

The new commits on the **master** branch must be included in the **build-history** branch. Since there is no development on the **build-history** branch, a **merge** command would always cause a fast forward merge, i.e., the **build-history** branch would simply refer to the current commit on the **master** branch.

Since we want to use the first-parent history on the **build-history** branch to retrieve the successful builds, we need to run **merge** with the **--no-ff** option.

```
> git merge --no-ff --no-commit origin/master
```

The parameters used in the **merge** command are

- **--no-ff:** Do no allow fast-forward merges.
- **--no-commit:** With this option, the merge is indeed performed on the workspace, but initially it is not committed. Only after successful building and running of the tests, a commit will be created.

Step 5: Do a build

Now the build server is used to build the current workspace and run tests. Git is not involved in this case. In the event of an error, the workflow is aborted and the build server informs the developers by email.

Step 6: Do a commit

If the build is successful, the prepared commit will be executed. The commit message should contain the build number assigned by the build server.

```
> git commit -m "build <build-nummer>"
```

If the build or tests failed, we can simply cancel at this point. In the next cycle, the workspace will be reset again (see Step 3).

Step 7: Mark the last successful build

The **last-build** branch on the central repository should always point to the last successfully built commit on the origin/master branch.

For this purpose, a local **last-build** branch is first created in the build repository or set to the correct commit. It is a little tricky to set this branch to the correct commit on the **origin/master** branch instead of on the merge commit on the current **build-history** branch.

You can see the various parents of a merge commit in Git marked by the **^-** notation: **^1** stands for the parent commit of the current branch, and **^2** for the parent commit of the added branch.

Take a look at commit **Z** In Figure 18.2. Its first parent is commit **Y** from the **build-history** branch, and its second parent is commit **D** from the **origin/master** branch.

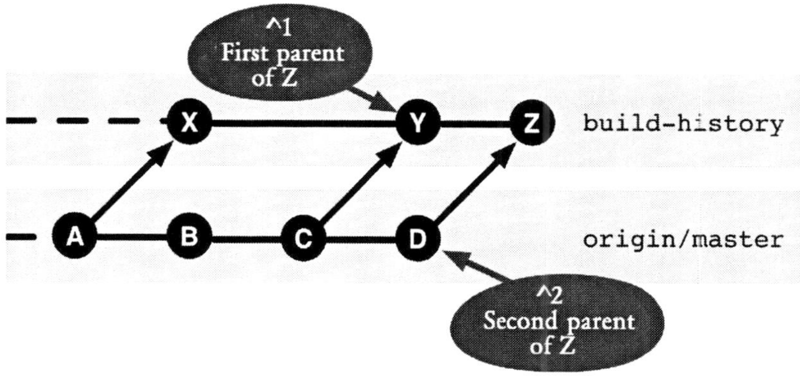

Figure 18.2: The build-history branch and the master branch

The following **branch** command creates a new **last-build** branch or modifies the existing branch so that it points to the commit from the **origin/master** branch:

```
> git branch --force last-build HEAD^2
```

The **--force** ensures that the **branch** command always creates a new **last-build** branch, even if one already exists.

The parameter **HEADˆ2** references the built commit on the **origin/master** branch.

After the branch points locally to the right commit, it must still be transmitted to the central repository. For this, use the **push** command.

```
> git push --force origin last-build:last-build
```

The parameters are as follows

--force: This option ensures that the local **last-build** branch is always displaced in the central repository with the new commit, even if the commit is not a successor of the last Last-Build commit.

origin: This parameter references the central repository.

last-build:last-build: This parameter indicates that the local **last-build** branch is transferred to the central **last-build** branch.

Comparing the Local Developer Version with the Last Successful Build

Every time there is a content error in a developer repository after a merge with the central repository, it is useful to compare the changes with respect to the last successful build.

The following section describes how you can compare your local version status with the last successfully built version on the build server.

Step 1: Check the central commit

First you should check if there are commits from other developers that are not yet successfully built in the central repository, because the error could come from someone else.

For this purpose, you can use the **log** command to determine whether there are commits in the central **origin/master** branch that are not yet included in the **origin/last-build** branch. In the example in Figure 18.3, you would find commit **C**.

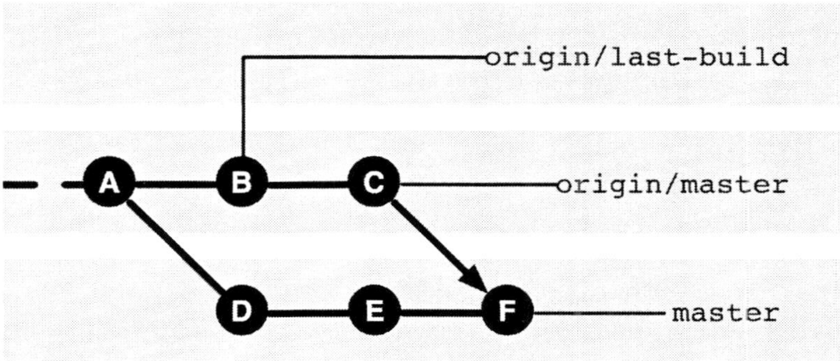

Figure 18.3: Using the last-build branch

```
> git log origin/last-build..origin/master
```

You can use the **diff** command to compare the changes.

```
> git diff origin/last-build origin/master
```

Step 2: Review the local commits

Next, you can check the changes in your own version compared to the last successful build.

```
> git diff origin/last-build
```

In the example in Figure 18.3, this would compare the contents of commit **F** with the contents of commit **B**. All changes in commits **C**, **D**, **E**, and **F** will be shown.

Troubleshooting with the Build History

In most cases, it is easy to find the location in the code that is causing an error. Often it is enough to read the description of the error in order to know at what point something must have gone wrong. Occasionally, however, errors creep in, which are difficult to find. Then it can be very helpful to know exactly when the error first appeared in the software. Since you can restore older versions of the software quickly with Git, it is possible to systematically isolate the error. You can start with an old version, in which the error is not occurring. Then you can get a later version and check whether the error occurs there. By repeating this in the version history you can find the commit in which the error first occurs. With any luck, the associated diff is small, and you have the error nailed very precisely.

However, the process can be quite a chore. Git therefore offers the **bisect** command that can help with this. The command finds the faulty commit by getting the "middle" commit enabled and tested in the affected area, and then proceed with the commit to the left or right of the last commit.

This method works most efficiently when it only has to consider versions that were previously built and tested successfully at least once. Otherwise, you would waste a lot of time with old versions that cannot be built due to serious errors.

Here, our build history comes into play, as it contains only commits that have been built successfully, and in which all unit tests have been successfully executed.

The build history, however, is not included in the local repository, nor is it present in the central repository of this branch. Using the **fetch** command, it is possible to import commits from other repositories.

Step 1: Link the build repository

To access the build repository, we create a remote named "build" in the developer repository.

```
> git remote add build <build-repo-url>
```

Step 2: Transfer the build history

Fetch the build history to the local developer repository using the **fetch** command.

```
> git fetch build
```

Step 3: Create a local branch

It is useful to create a local branch that is based on the **build-history** branch.

```
> git checkout -b history build/build-history
```

Step 4: Do a bisect

Define a suitable initial "good" commit and start debugging with the **bisect** command.

```
> git bisect start HEAD <good-commit>
```

Git will now select a "middle" commit for testing. We perform our test and depending on the results define the current commit as "good" or "bad."

```
> git bisect good
```

or

```
> git bisect bad
```

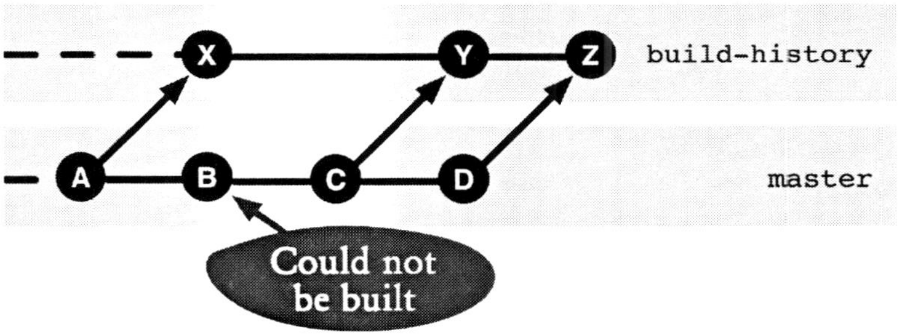

Figure 18.4: Troubleshooting with bisect

Since Git looks at merge commits at both parents, it may happen that the chosen commit does not come from our **build-history** branch. Figure 18.4 shows a typical commit history. If the algorithm that Git employs checks the commits between commit **X** and commit **Z**, then commits **B** to **D** can be selected from the **master** branch.

Step 5: interpret the results

After a successful bisection process the faulty commit is found in the build history. Behind every commit in the build history, however, several commits on the **master** branch can pop (see commit **Y** in Figure 18.4). To print the log messages of the possible faulty commits, a little acrobatics needs to be done again.

The second parent (**^2**) of each build commit always corresponds to a commit on the **master** branch. The first parent (**^1**) of a build commit corresponds to the previous build commit.

The following **log** command determines, on the basis of a "faulty" build commit, all commits on the **master** branch that could have led to the error:

```
> git log <bad-commit>^1^2..<bad-commit>^2
```

If commit **Y** in Figure 18.4 has been identified as defective, then the **log** command would show commits **B** and **C** as a possible cause of the error.

Step 6: Clean up

After the **bisect** command has been completed, all unnecessary branches, commits, and remotes can be removed from the developers repository:

```
> git bisect reset

> git checkout master

> git branch -D build-history

> git remote rm build
```

Why Not the Alternatives?

Why No Tags?

An alternative implementation of the build history would be to store successful builds rather than merge commits in a separate branch as tags. This would even make the process simpler as you do not have to prepare and perform merge commits. The following are points to consider:

- It would create a lot of tags, and the non-build tags would be hard to find.
- The more efficient troubleshooting with bisection only on commits that can be built and successfully tested would not be possible.
- The logical order of the builds (tags) would implicitly manifested only by the build number.

Also for the **last-build** branch we could use a tag instead of the branch. This would require the tag to be deleted and recreated after each successful build. This works in a local repository, but once a tag has been transferred to the central repository, there will be problems.

While it is still possible to delete and recreate a tag centrally, all clones will not get the updated tag by calling the **pull** command as it would ignore any existing tags.

Why not Put the Build History in the Central Repository?

In the implementation described, the build history will not be published in the central repository, but will only be visible in the build repository.

Why will it make no sense to store the build history in the central repository?

The main reason is that otherwise the normal commit history would be “defaced” through the many merge commits. Every successful build enforces a new merge commit, based on the **origin/master** branch and **build-history** branch. In the normal viewing of a project history, it is irrelevant which version was built successfully. The merge commits would leave the log output appear cluttered.

The worst thing of all is if there are multiple build servers instead of one. For example because both the **master** branch and the **codefreeze** branch would be built, there would be more build commits in the central repository.

The beauty of the lattice approach is that it is always possible to bring together the commits in the build history and the normal project commits in a repository. For this purpose, a fetch, both from the central repository and the build repository, is performed.

Chapter 19
Performing A Release

For each project or product, there is time where a release needs to be created. This process differs from one company or organization to another.

Git does not specify when it comes to the release process. With tags and branches, however, Git provides powerful tools that support a very wide range of release processes.

This workflow describes an example of a release process for a typical web project. In our web project, there are always a productive release and a future release. In a productive release major bugs and security risks are resolved very quickly (in the so-called hotfixes). This new release is run through a detailed multi-day test period (code freeze phase) before being published. At the same time, development for the next release can proceed.

This workflow shows how a release process can be implemented for a project with Git, such that

- Hotfixes are supported on the productive release,
- Parallel work on a new release during the code freeze phase is possible
- It is guaranteed that all errors that were fixed as hotfixes or during the test phase, flow back to development,
- The history of releases and hotfixes is easy to access, and

- Comparisons between releases and development versions can be done easily

Overview

Figure 19.1 shows the branches required for the development and release process.

The development takes place on the **master** branch. It does not matter whether or not feature branches are used. It is only important that the **master** branch contains the code that should lead to the next release.

During the release preparation, a separate **codefreeze** branch is used to stabilize the future release. At the same time, development on the **master** branch for the next release can proceed.

Once the stabilization is completed, a release commit is created on the stable branch and simultaneously a release tag is generated.

If a fatal error occurs in the productive release, a new hot fix branch will be created. After troubleshooting, a hotfix commit is performed on the stable branch and a release tag is created.

The **codefreeze** branch and the **hotfix** branch exist only so long as the stabilizing or troubleshooting takes place.

The changes during the stabilization and the hotfix will always be returned through merges with the **master** branch.

Requirements

Only one productive release: There is only one productive release, i.e., there are not multiple versions of the product or project maintained. Git can handle multiple versions but this workflow is designed to deal with one productive release.

Stable development: The development branch is well tested and the expected errors in the code freeze phase are manageable so that this can be completed in a few days.

Full release: New things and changes on the development branch always go into the next release.

Workflow "Performing A Release"

A release is created for a project. The preparation for the release takes place in a separate branch. Fixes can be done on the productive release.

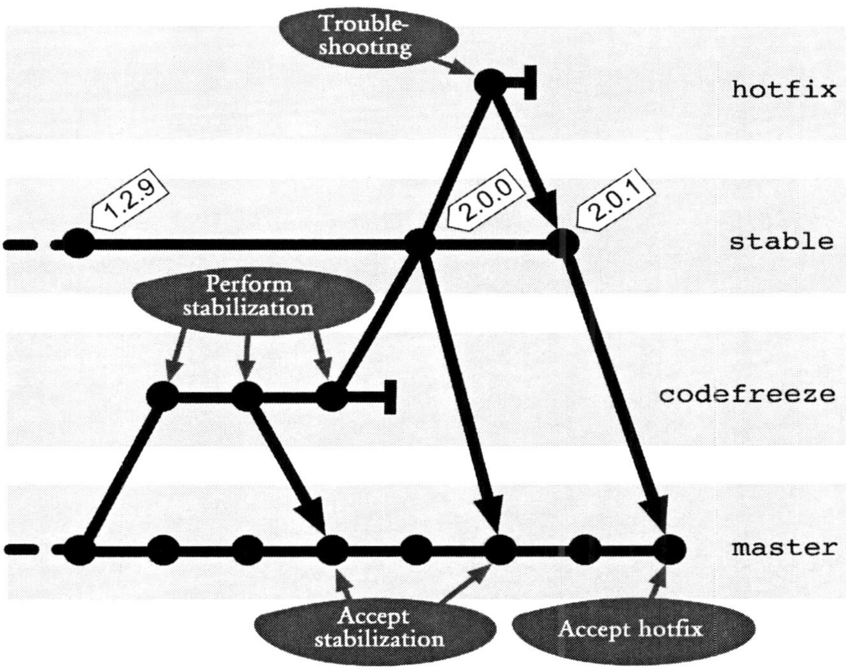

Figure 19.1: Workflow overview

Process and Implementation

Preparation: Creating a stable branch

The following section describes the unique preparation of the repository to perform a release.

This workflow requires a branch named **stable**. This branch should contain only commits that represent a new release or a hotfix release. The first-parent history of the **stable** branch can be used as the release history, which can be displayed using the **log** command.

```
> git checkout stable

> git log --first-parent -oneline

5901ec9 Hotfix-Release-2.0.1
b955c9c Release-2.0.0
5d0173d Release-1.0.0
3a05e26 init
```

The following are the parameters used in the command.

--first-parent: Only the first parent is considered.
--oneline: Only one line of the log output is printed.

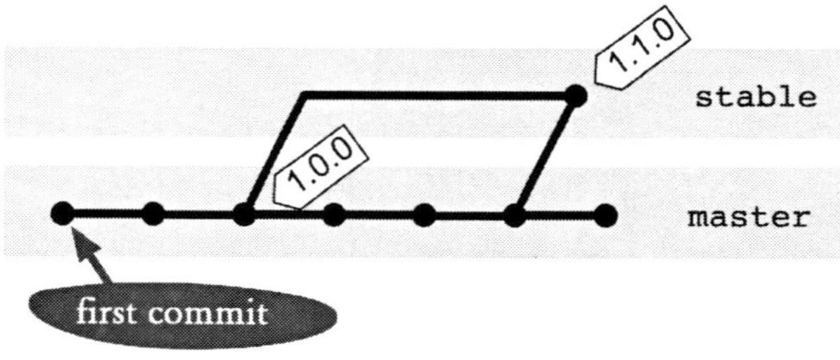

Figure 19.2: Starting the first release

It is important to define the beginning of the **stable** branch correctly. If the **stable** branch will be created at the first release commit, then the previous commits of the **master** branch must be included in the first-parent history (See Figure 19.2).

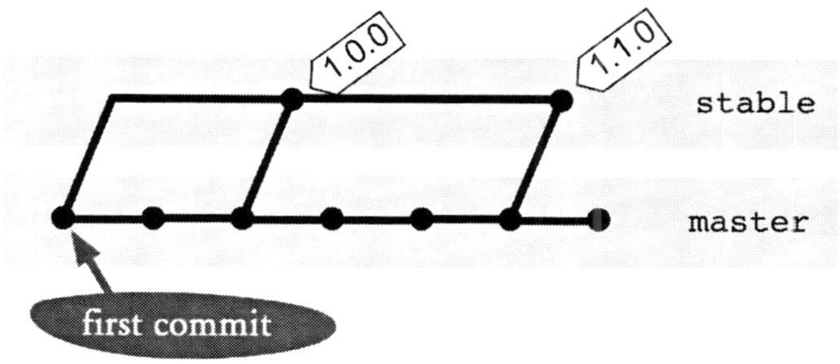

Figure 19.3: Starting the stable branch with the first commit

It is better to start the **stable** branch at the first commit of the **master** branch. This way, only one unnecessary commit will be included in the release history (see the first commit in Figure 19.3).

Step 1: Determine the first commit

Unfortunately, there is no Git command that can be used to find the first commit of a branch. The best way is to display the log and look for the last entry.

```
> git log --oneline --first-parent | tail -1

3a05e26 init
```

The parameters used in the command are as follows.

- **--oneline:** Only prints one line of the output.
- **--first-parent:** Returns only the first parent of each commit. This leads to using fewer resources and thus a faster result.
- **| tail -1:** Prints only the last line of the log output.

Step 2: Creating a stable branch

After the first commit is found, the **stable** branch can be created. With the **branch** command, additional branch names can also be specified.

```
> git branch stable 3a05e26
```

Prepare and Create A Release

The following section describes the steps needed to release a project with Git.

Project development takes place on the **master** branch. On this branch, the necessary unit tests and integration tests are also performed.

When the development is complete and the project is ready to be released, normally more and more intensive tests need to be performed. This phase is commonly referred to as "code freeze." This means that only code for release-critical bug fixes and their possible workarounds will be implemented. How long this phase lasts depends largely on the development process. This can range from the existing code quality and the tests. It can take a few hours or several weeks.

This should not stop the development for the next release during the code freeze phase, as the stabilization of the release is performed in a separate **codefreeze** branch. This branch exists only until the new release has been stabilized. The next time you create a release, a new **codefreeze** branch will be created.

Step 1: Create a codefreeze branch

The **codefreeze** branch is created based on the current **master** branch. The **checkout** command can be used to create the new branch and activate it.

```
> git checkout -b codefreeze master
```

Step 2: stabilize with the codefreeze branch

In the **codefreeze** branch, only errors that are preventing a release will be corrected. The fix is carried out according to the principle of minimal change. If there is no simple solution to the minimal error, a workaround is implemented if necessary.

The new commits on the **codefreeze** branch must be regularly merged to the **master** branch. These one-off fixes will also be eliminated from the current development.

```
> git checkout master

> git merge codefreeze
```

Workarounds should be incorporated in the **codefreeze** branch, as these will be retained in the **master** branch. In the **master** branch workarounds can be reverted (for example, using the **revert** command) and a better implementation created (see Figure 19.4).

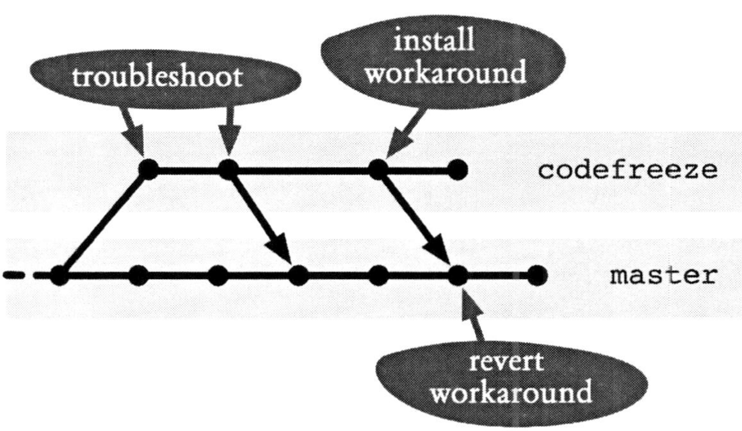

Figure 19.4: Dealing with bug fixes and workarounds

Step 3: Create a release

After the **codefreeze** branch has been successfully tested, the release can be created.

As such, a merge from the **codefreeze** branch must be carried out on the **stable** branch. It is important that in the **stable** branch there are no commits that have not been tested on the **codefreeze** branch. Such commits would lead to a merge such that there is a major release in the **stable** branch that has not been tested in this compilation.

The following **log** command checks if there are commits in the **stable** branch that are missing in the **codefreeze** branch. No output means there are no new commits in the **stable** branch.

```
> git log codefreeze..stable --oneline
```

If the **log** command returns an output, a renewed merge from the **stable** branch to the **codefreeze** branch and the tests necessary for the release must be done again.

If the log output is empty, the merge of the **codefreeze** branch can be performed in the **stable** branch.

Normally, Git would do a fast-forward merge in this merge, because we have ensured that there are no new commits in the **stable** branch. However, to obtain a meaningful first-parent history on the **stable** branch, use the **--no-ff** option. You should also use a comment that clearly identifies the new commits for the release.

```
> git checkout stable

> git merge codefreeze --no-ff -m "Release-2.0.0"
```

The **--no-ff** option indicates that the **merge** command should not perform a fast-forward merge, i.e., it will always create a new commit.

In addition to the commit, a new tag for the release should be created. The tag can be used to quickly access the release commit, e.g. to be used by the **diff** command.

```
> git tag -a release-2.0.0 -m "Release-2.0.0"
```

Finally, the **codefreeze** branch will be deleted as this branch is only used to stabilize and will be recreated in the next release.

```
> git branch -d codefreeze
```

Step 4: Update the master branch

Now that the release was performed to guarantee that any changes in the release are also included in the **master** branch.

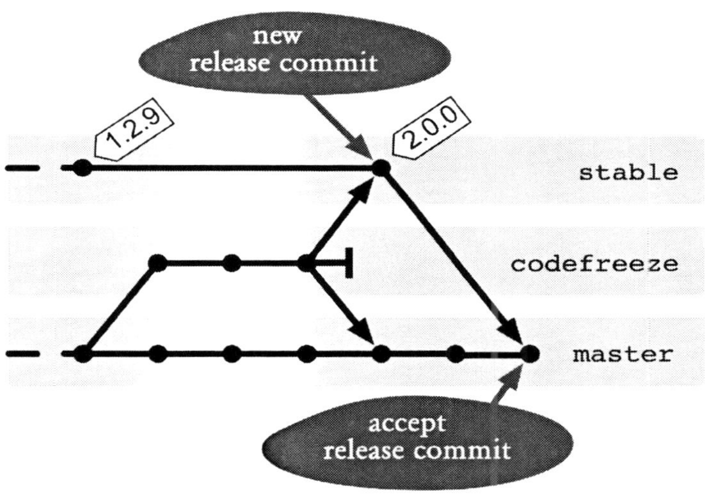

Figure 19.5: Performing a release

Although all bug fix commits in the **codefreeze** branch are already merged into the **master** branch, the new release commit still exists (see Figure 19.5). Although this release commit does not change any files and is therefore irrelevant to the **master** branch, queries such as "Which commit is in the **stable** branch, but not in the **master** branch?" would show regularly. Therefore, the **stable** branch needs to be merged with the **master** branch.

```
> git checkout master

> git merge stable -m "Nach Release-2.0.0"
```

Thus, from the perspective of version management, the new release has been completely created.

Creating A Hotfix

A hotfix is an urgent change that is supposed to be as fast as possible and independent from other changes. A hotfix is implemented directly against the version of the current release. Less important errors in a web application will typically be rectified in the next release. However, a mistake that makes it impossible to work with the system or that can lead to security risks, must be corrected immediately.

Step 1: Create a hotfix branch and troubleshoot

The error correction takes place on a separate **hotfix** branch. In order to enable parallel processing of multiple hotfixes, everyone gets their own branch.

The starting point is the **stable** branch, which points to the last productive release.

```
> git checkout -b hotfix-a1 stable
```

Now the necessary changes for the project can be made.

Step 2: Verify that parallel hotfixes have taken place

If the error is corrected and a new release should be created, you must check the commit history to see if there was another hotfix in the meantime. To do this, use the **log** command to find commits that are in the **stable** branch, but not in the **hotfix** branch.

```
> git log hotfix-a1..stable --oneline
```

If in the meantime there were other changes in the **stable** branch, before the hotfix can be installed, you have to check if the other changes will work with the hotfix. So that the history will remain linear, the hotfix should be placed as the last commit of the **stable** branches by rebasing (see Figure 19.6).

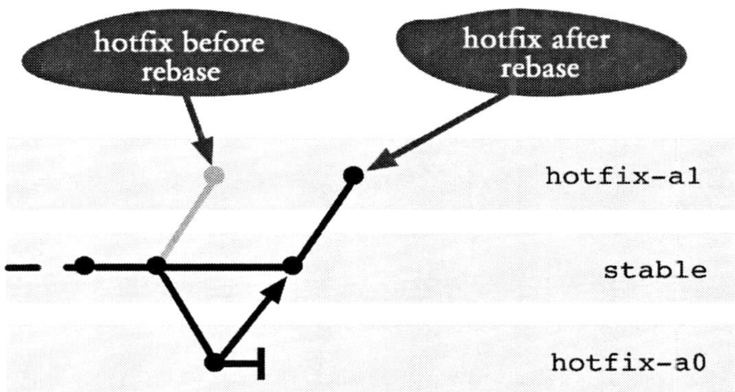

Figure 19.6: Rebasing the hotfix branch

```
> git rebase stable
```

Now the hotfix commits are based on the last commit of the **stable** branch.

Step 3: Release the hotfix

In order to officially release the hotfix, the **hotfix** branch has to be merged with the **stable** branch. Again a fast-forward merge is not allowed in order to create a new commit. The merge comment should be used to specify the necessary release information.

```
> git checkout stable
```

```
> git merge hotfix-a1 --no-ff -m "Hotfix-Release-2.0.1"
```

In addition to the commit, a new tag will be created for the release.

```
> git tag -a release-2.0.1 -m "Hotfix-Release 2.0.1"
```

Finally, you can delete the **hotfix** branch.

Step 4: Accept hotfix changes in another branch

Errors that were fixed with a **hotfix** branch must be transferred to the other active branch.

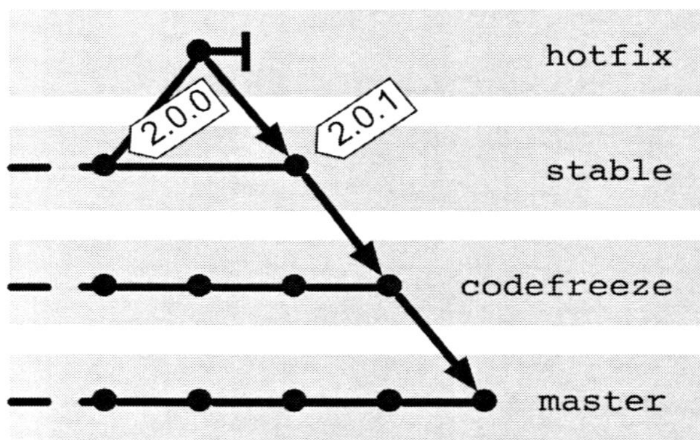

Figure 19.7: Accepting hotfixes in the codefreeze and master branches

During a code freeze phase, the hotfix must be brought to the **codefreeze** branch only. Then, the changes in the **codefreeze** branch are transferred to the **master** branch (see Figure 19.7).

```
> git checkout codefreeze

> git merge stable -m "Hotfix 2.0.1"

> git checkout master

> git merge codefreeze -m "Hotfix 2.0.1"
```

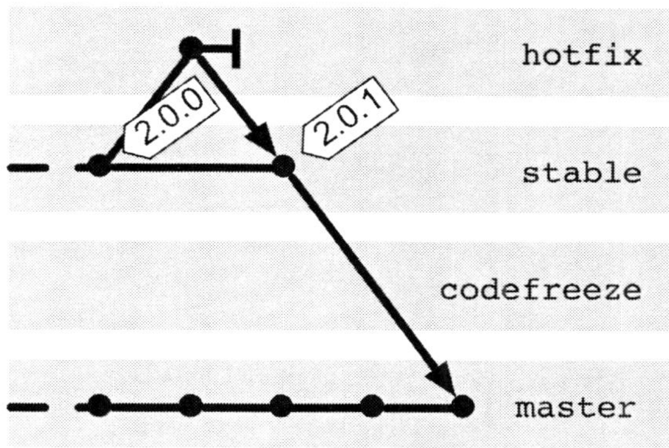

Figure 19.8: Accepting hotfixes in the master branch

During a non-code freeze phase, the changes are transferred directly to the **master** branch (see Figure 19.8).

```
> git checkout master
> git merge stable -m "Hotfix 2.0.1"
```

Why Not the Alternatives?

Why Not with Tags Only?

In the workflow described a **stable** branch and additional tags for identifying the releases are used. Would tags only be insufficient?

For pure marking and thus reproducing the releases, the use of rich tags would actually be sufficient.

However, when it comes to understanding the history of releases and hotfix releases, then tags alone are impractical. You could only guess based on the tag name in chronological order. With a **stable** branch, you can use the first-parent history.

Why Not Do without Tags?

Tags are symbolic names for commits. If you want to compare the current development version with a particular release (using the **diff** command), then tags are more practical than commit hashes.

```
> git diff release-1.0.0
```

If you were to eliminate the tags, you would first have to search for the right commit in the **stable** branch and then specify the hash.

```
> git diff 5d0173d
```

Why No Fast-Forward Merges?

In Git, branches are only references to commits. If a branch is activated (using the **checkout** command), then the reference to each new commit is automatically updated. There is no historical information on which commit was created on which branch. The only "heuristic" option is to use the first-parent history of a branch.

A fast-forward merge results in two branches pointing to the same commit. If the first-parent history is used, it is no longer traceable in which of the two branches the previous commit was created.

If you do not allow fast-forward merges, a new commit is always created. The first parent points to the last commit in the current branch and the second parent to the added commit.

Why Not Implement A Hotfix Directly on the stable Branch?

The workflow describes that for correcting a serious error, a separate **hotfix** branch should be created. In principle, it would also be possible to work directly on the **stable** branch.

However, under certain circumstances, commits with no associated releases would appear in the first-parent history of the **stable** branch. This happens when more than one commit must be created for a hotfix.

Also, the parallel creation of hotfixes can be difficult.

Chapter 20
Splitting A Large Project

Often a software project begins as a small monolithic system. During development the project and the team are growing larger. Modularization is becoming increasingly important. At first the internal structure of the project is modularized. Eventually, you would like to develop individual modules separately and submit your own release cycle.

Since Git repositories are always versioned as a whole, a new Git repository must be created for each separate release module.

The challenge of modularization of a Git repository is to take as much as possible of the old file versions in the new repository. At the same time the new repository should not contain any files that are not used within the module. Also not required are commits in which no changes were made to any file in the module.

In the main repository, the history of the module is not removed so that older project versions can be reproduced. As a consequence, the historical data of the separated module is located in both repositories.

Most of the separated modules will still be needed from the main project and should be integrated as external modules. For this type of integration, there is the submodule concept in Git.

This workflow shows how you can extract a module with Git so that

- only files required by the module are transferred to a new repository,
- the history of the module files will remain in the new repository, and
- the module can be integrated again as an external submodule.

Overview

For the following procedure, we use a project structure as shown in the top section of Figure 20.1.

The example for this workflow is based on a Java directory structure. There are three modules in the project as a whole. The files in each module are located in the **src** and **test** subdirectories. In other words, a module in each case consists of two separate parts. The third module, **module3**, is separated into a separate Git repository.

As a first step, you need to remove all unnecessary files and commits from a clone of the original repository using the **filter branch** command. Subsequently, the directory structure of the new module repository is updated. Finally, the **module3** module is removed from the main project and the new module repository is incorporated again as a submodule in the external directory. The result will look like the bottom section of Figure 20.1.

In the new module repository it will be possible to reconstruct the historical changes to files, that is, to track who changed what and when. However, it is usually not possible to reproduce old versions completely. The reason is that a module often emerges from files of other modules. If you tried to restore an old version of the project from the module repository, there would be a patchwork of files in different directories. In addition, in the past, the module might have been determined as a dependency of other files that are not longer available.

In the main repository, old versions of the entire project, including the module files, are still recoverable.

Requirements

Internal modularization: The project has been modularized internally, i.e., there is a module that can be developed and versioned separately.

Module files are located in a few directories: When extracting the old versions of the module, files in each directory must be treated separately. If the files are very scattered, the cost is very large.

Workflow "Splitting A Large Project"

A module is removed from a project and migrated to a separate repository. The commit history will be preserved, unnecessary files and commits will be removed. The separated module is brought back as an external submodule.

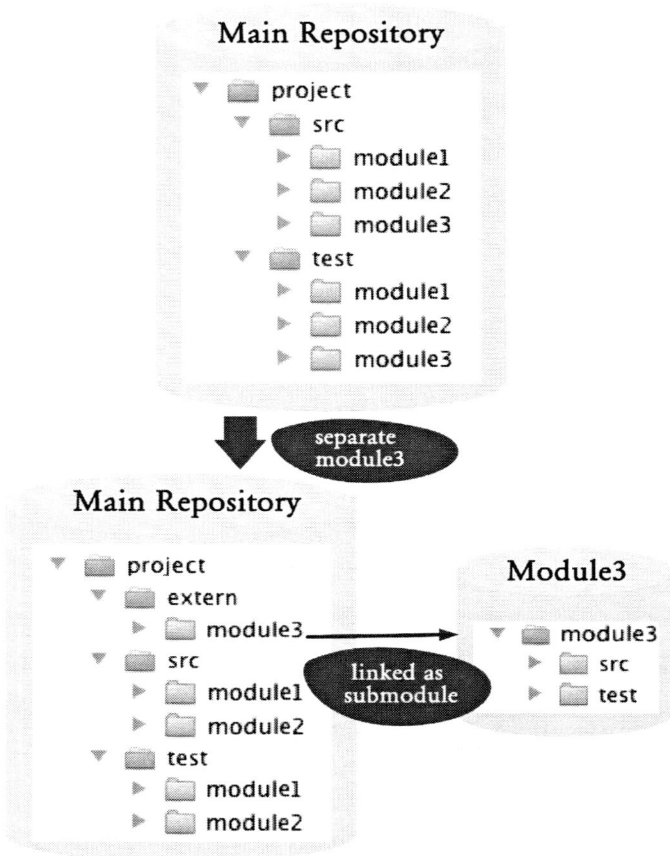

Figure 20.1: Workflow overview

Process and Implementation

Warning! Some of the following commands change the repository very fundamentally. Although in Git it is often possible to undo changes, you should make sure to back up your repository before you start with the next steps.

```
> git clone --no-hardlinks --bare projekt.git projekt.backup.git
```

The **--no-hardlinks** option guarantees that the cloned repository and the original repository to do not share any files.

Separating the Module Repository

Step 1: Clone the main repository

As a starting point for the module repository, create a copy of the main repository.

```
> git clone --no-hardlinks --bare projekt.git modul3-work.git
```

Step 2: Remove unnecessary files and commits

Next, unnecessary files and commits must be removed. This is the most complex step and vital to the preservation of history.

To remove the content of a repository content, use the **filter branch** command. This creates a new commit for each existing commit. By varying the filter, the new commits can be changed.

The following **filter branch** command removes the **src/module1** directory from the commit.

```
> cd module3

> git filter-branch --force --index-filter
    'git rm -r --cached --ignore-unmatch src/module1'
    --tag-name-filter cat
    --prune-empty -- --all
```

The parameters used are as follows.

-index-filter 'git rm -r -cached -ignore-unmatch ...':
With this option, files can be removed from a commit. The **rm** command is called for each commit. In our example, we remove the **src/module1** directory. If your project does not have a very modular structure, you may need to delete more files and directories .

-tag-name-filter cat: This option creates tags for existing or new commits.
-prune-empty: This option removes all commits that contain no files in the previous filter.
-all: This option applies the filter to all branches in the project.

For the example project, we have to invoke the command repeatedly on the **test/module1**, **src/module2** and **test/module2** directories.

For the exact descriptions of all the options of the **filter branch** command, please refer to the Git help.

Step 3: Remove unnecessary branches and tags

Not all tags and branches in the module repository are useful. For instance, the tags and branches that have no relation to the extracted module are useless. The unnecessary branches and tags should be removed.

```
> git tag -d v1.0.1
```

```
> git branch -D v2.0_bf
```

Step 4: Scale down the module repository

In order for Git to remove all unnecessary files from its internal management data, a repeated cloning is required.

```
> git clone --no-hardlinks
--bare module3-work.git module3.git
```

The previous module repository **module3-work.git** is no longer needed and can be deleted.

```
> rm -rf modul3-work.git
```

Step 5: Customize the directory structure of the repository module

So far, the directory structure of the new module repository looks the same as that of the main project. Only the unnecessary modules are missing. The adaptation of the directory structure can now be done through normal file operations. For this purpose, a clone with a workspace is necessary.

```
> git clone module3.git module3
```

The **src/module3** directory is renamed **src** and the **test/module3** directory **test**.

```
> cd module3
> mv src/module3 module3
> rmdir src
> mv module3 src
> mv test/module3 module3
> rmdir test
> mv module3 test
```

Subsequently, the changes are normally confirmed with the **commit** command and transferred to the bare repository with the **push** command.

```
> git add --all
> git commit -m "Directory structure adapted"
> git push
```

If there are other branches in the module repository, the file operations must be performed on all branches.

It often makes little sense to take the branches of the main project. The module starts a new release cycle, and the old branches are uninteresting.

Step 6: Remove the module directory from the main repository

After the separated module has been migrated to a separate repository, in the next steps the main repository is adapted. The now unnecessary directories of the separated module, **src/module3** and **test/module3**, must be removed. The adaptation is quite normal at the file level in a clone of the main repository.

If there are other branches in the project, which should be adapted to the new structure, the changes need to be made there as well. The **cherry-pick** command can be used to transfer the changes automatically into several branches.

Integrating A Module Repository as An External Repository

After the previous sequence, there are now two separate repositories. Normally, the main project will continue to require the separated module, so an integration is necessary.

The integration options depend very strongly on the development platform used. So in a Java Maven project, you would build the separated module individually and store the resulting artifacts in a Maven repository. The main project would define the artifacts as dependencies and during the build get them from the Maven repository.

If you want to perform the integration with Git, the concept of submodules is available. With submodules, directories in a Git repository can be linked with other Git repositories.

Step 1: Integrate an external module into the main repository

In our example, we want to integrate the repository of **module3** in the **extern/module3** directory of the main project. The starting point is a clone of the main repository. We decide on the root directory of the project and add it to the module repository using the **submodule add** command. The first parameter is the path or URL to the module repository, and the second parameter is the future directory in the repository:

```
> git submodule add /global-path-to/module3.git extern/module3
```

The **submodule add** command creates a clone of the external repository in the specified directory. In addition, it is recorded in the current repository that the directory references an external repository.

The **extern/module3** directory now points to the latest commit (**HEAD**) of the external repository.

Still, the submodule is only visible in the workspace. Only by using the **commit** command will the changes be reflected in the repository:

```
> git add -all
```

```
> git commit -m "Modul3 added"
```

You can use the **push** command to transfer the submodule shortcut to the central repository.

Why Not the Alternatives?

Why Not Use A New Repository?

An alternative to this workflow would be to simply create a new repository for the module. Thus, there would be no project history of the module in the new repository. It would also be possible to find the old versions in the main repository.

As long as this limitation does not bother you, this solution is very easy to implement.

Why Not Use --subdirectory-filter?

This workflow uses the **filter-branch** command with **--index-filter**. This allows you to remove files from commits.

The **--subdirectory-filter** option of the **filter-branch** command removes all files except the specified directory. In addition, it removes the selected directory on the new root of the repository.

As long as the module to be separated resides in exactly one directory, this command is easy to use. In this example, however, the module is divided into two directories, and thus could not be used with this filter.

Even if individual files of the module were formerly in other directories or the module directory has been renamed, **subdirectory-filter** would only import the history incompletely.

Chapter 21
Merging Small Projects

In the initial phase of a project, prototypes for critical design decisions and technologies are often implemented. When the evaluation is complete, you would want to combine the successful prototypes to form the first version of the overall project.

In such a scenario, the prototypes are often versioned in separate repositories. Once the entire project is started, a common repository is preferred, i.e., the files of the various prototypes need to be merged.

In another scenario, initially projects were too modularized and versioned in different repositories. It later turns out that often simultaneous changes are made and files often need to be moved between repositories. In this case too, is a single repository useful.

The workflow in this chapter shows how multiple repositories can be merged with Git so that

- the histories of all files and
- the tags of all repositories are kept.

Overview

This workflow is based on Git's ability to import commits from different remote repositories to a repository using the **fetch** command. Git does not require that the commits to be imported have a common origin.

The top section of Figure 21.1 shows two repositories named **backend** and **ui** that will be used as examples.

After importing the commits to a repository, there are two separate commit histories. If you switch between commits in the backend project and the ui project, then only the files of the selected project will be displayed in the workspace.

The important step towards a common project version is to merge the independent commit histories using the **merge** command.

In preparation for the merge, it makes sense to create a new root directory for each of the projects and move all the existing files to this directory (the new directories are **backend** and **ui**). After the merge, the root directory of the common project will contain two subdirectories (**backend** and **ui**) (see the bottom section of Figure 21.1).

This approach will prevent conflicts during a merge.

Requirement

Different tag names: Each project must use a unique tag name, i.e., you cannot have identical tags in different repositories. If there are identical tags, you must delete these tags or add new tags with a unique name.

Workflow "Merging Small Projects"

Several projects, each with a separate repository, are merged into a common repository. The commit histories of the projects must remain.

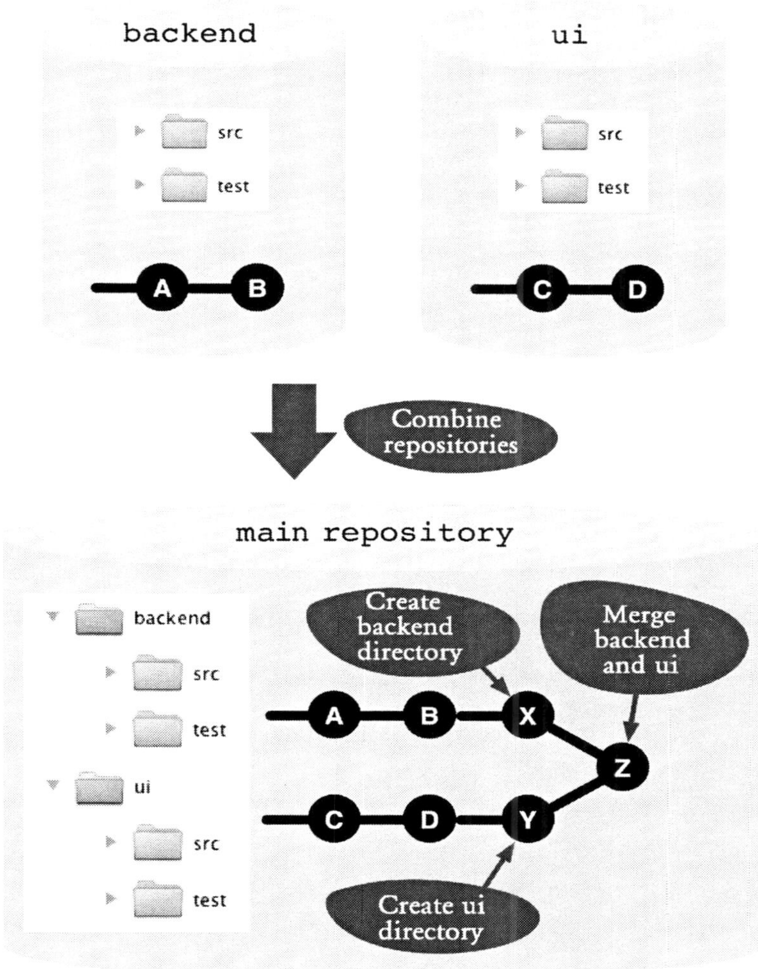

Figure 21.1: Workflow overview

Process and Implementation

Combine Repositories

In the following sequence we use two repositories (**ui** and **backend**) as an example. Each repository has a **master** branch. As a result, we want to merge both into a single repository that only has one **master** branch.

Step 1: Create a main repository

First, the new common repository is created as a clone of the backend repository and switched to the new workspace.

```
> git clone backend common
```

```
> cd common
```

Step 2: Move the files in the project directory (first repository)

So that merging with another project does not cause file conflicts, create a new folder.

```
> mkdir backend
```

Then, move all files to the new directory. To do this, use the **mv** command. This moves files and directories at the operating system level and at the same time performs the necessary **add** and **rm** commands to take the changes into the next commit:

```
> git mv src test backend
```

Finally, complete the changes with the **commit** command.

```
> git commit -m "backend directory created"
```

Step 3: Import the second repository

To import the **ui** repository, we create a new remote in the common repository.

```
> cd common
> git remote add ui ../ui/
```

Using the **fetch** command, import all the Git objects (branches, tags, commits) from the **ui** repository into the common repository.

```
> git fetch ui
```

Attention! If there is a tag name in the **ui** repository that already exists in the common repository, it will be ignored.

Step 4: Move the files to the project directory

Next, create a new project directory named **ui** from the imported UI project. Since the name of the branch in the UI project is also **master**, and this name is already used by the branch from the backend project, you have to choose another name (**uimaster**) for the local branch.

```
> git checkout -b uimaster ui/master
```

The parameters used are as follows.

-b: A new branch must be created and activated.
uimaster: The name of the local branch.
ui/master: The reference to the **master** branch in the remote of the **ui** repository.

The creation of the project directory and the moving of the files are the same as Step 2

```
> mkdir ui
> git mv src test ui
> git commit -m "ui directory created"
```

Step 5: Merge the projects

After both projects were imported into the common repository and each is in its own project directory, a merge is performed.

The merge will take place on the **master** branch, so this branch needs to be activated.

```
> git checkout master
```

With the **merge** command, the **uimaster** branch is merged with the **master** branch. Since both projects have different project directories, there may not be merge conflicts.

```
> git merge uimaster
```

The result of the merge operation can be shown with the "graphical" **log** command. It is good to see that the commits of the two original projects are developed independently from each.

```
> git log --graph --oneline

* e40fcb2 Merge branch 'uimaster'
|\
| \\
| * ace51c9 ui directory created
| * 40feb24 foo and bar added
* f8bd134 backend directory created
* fa1482a bar added
* bddfa53 foo added
```

The **uimaster** branch can now be deleted, since it was only needed temporarily for the merge.

```
> git branch -d uimaster
```

That's it. Now there is a common repository that includes the histories and tags of both project repositories.

Why Not the Alternatives?

Why Not Do without New Project Directories?

Can we skip Steps 2 and 4? Why do we have to move the project files to their own directories?

If you do not create the new directories, the **merge** command will try to merge the root directories of both projects and their files. Existing files will be combined and conflicts will have to resolved.

If you are merging two previously independent projects, it makes sense in the rarest of cases to combine files with the same name. In most cases you will want to rename or move a file. This is easier to perform directly at the file level than in the middle of a merge operation.

The procedure described shows it is possible to merge files by creating new module directories and then versioning them.

Chapter 22 Outsourcing Long Histories

Git repositories tend to become large over time, despite its efficient memory management. This effect is usually negligible if the source files are the only items versioned in the repository. The size of such a repository is not tiny compared to current hard disks and network bandwidth.

However, if large binary files (libraries, release artifacts, test databases, images) are also versioned, the repository size can indeed attract negative attention.

Compared to a centralized version control system, a distributed version control system tends to consume more resources. When you clone a repository, all historical files will also be copied.

This workflow describes how you can outsource the history of a Git repository so that

- the new project repository uses less resources and
- it is still possible to do a search with the old commits using the **log**, **blame** and **annotate** commands.

Overview

This workflow has three pillars:

grafts file: With the **grafts** file, commit parents in the local repository can be deleted.

filter-branch command: The **filter-branch** command can copy all commits from a repository and modify them. The modified parent relationship can be removed permanently.

alternates file: With the **alternates** file, commits from other repositories can be merged.

The top section of Figure 22.1 outlines our project repository. There are three commits: **A**, **B** and **C**. The history of **C** needs to be removed.

First, with the help of the **grafts** file, we remove the parents of commit **C**. A new project repository is created and then treated with the **filter-branch** command, which only includes the modified commit **C**. This outsourcing is now done. The development now takes place only on the new project history. The previous project repository now only serves as an archive.

To perform searches in the whole history, the archive repository is linked from the new project repository using the **alternates** file. With the **grafts** file, commit **C** is assigned the historically correct parent (see the bottom section of Figure 22.1).

Requirements

Coordinated break: All team members must agree on a simultaneous break from the repository, and then continue working on the new clone.

History is rarely needed: If the historical information is needed very often and by many developers, then it makes more sense to accept the larger resource consumption.

Commit hashes do not matter: Git can use commit hashes to detect unauthorized changes to old versions.

However, this workflow breaks the history and creates new commits.

Workflow “Outsourcing Long Histories”

This workflow aims to reduce the size of a repository that contains a very long commit history with many large files. The older commits are outsourced to a separate repository. Searching the history is still possible.

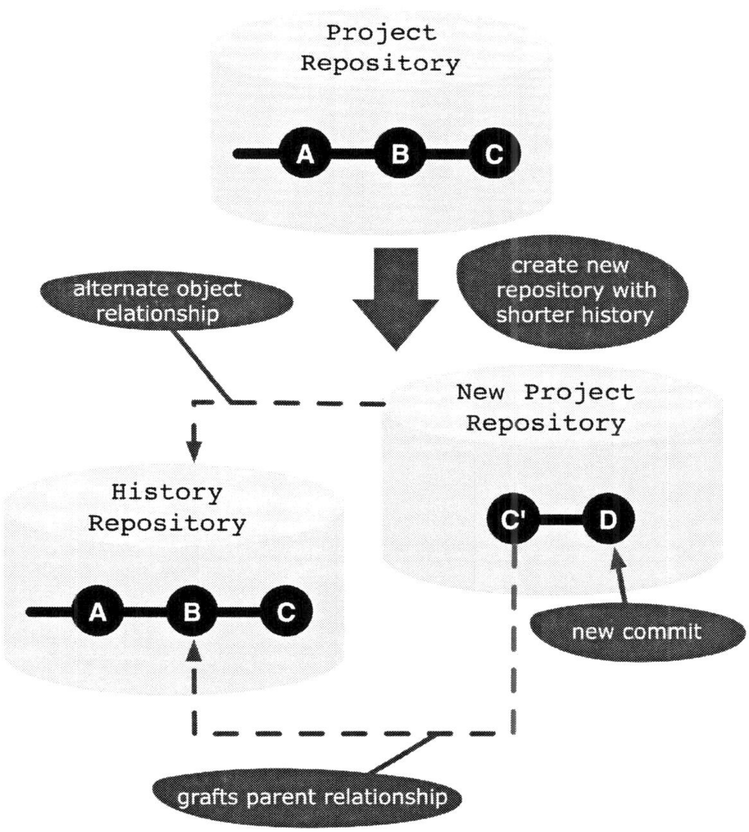

Figure 22.1: Workflow overview

Process and Implementation

Outsourcing the History

This procedure describes in detail how the history of a repository can be outsourced. More specifically, a new repository is created which only contains the truncated history.

Attention! Clones of the old repository will not work with the new repository. Therefore, any development changes must be merged to the central repository before the next steps. All developers must be informed that no further changes can be made in the clones.

The starting point is shown in the top section of Figure 22.1. The example is based on a bare repository with three commits from the **master** branch. A new project repository with commit **C** must be created.

For the following steps we need the complete hashes of commits **C** and **B**. This can be determined using the following **log** command:

```
> cd project.git

> git log --pretty=oneline

166a7e047a85b318720dc6e857a5321f9a3df7b4 C
dcbddd5cd590de3d30e1ecca1882c9187e7eab95 B
577b8e2cf613c43ed969453477fadc189482c1fb A
```

The **--pretty=oneline** parameter specifies the log output should be printed in a single line. Unlike the **--oneline** parameter, the full hash value is returned.

Step 1: Create a grafts tag

This step is a preparation for integrating the future archive repository. To integrate the archive, you will need to know the hash of the last historical predecessor commit. In our case, this is commit **B**. An elegant solution to permanently store this information is to create a tag (**grafts/master**) at the new “first” commit (commit **C**) and store the hash in the tag comment. This tag will be present in the future project repository. It makes no sense to create a tag at commit **B**, as this will not be included in the new project repository.

The **tag** command gets the hash of commit C passed, and the hash of commit **B** stored in the tag description.

```
> git tag -a grafts/master
166a7e047a85b318720dc6e857a5321f9a3df7b4
-m "Predecessor: dcbddd5cd590de3d30e1ecca1882c9187e7eab95"
```

Here, **grafts/master** is the name of the new tag. In Git, it is possible to create a tag and branch name hierarchy by using the / symbol.

If you have multiple branches, then you have to perform the above step for all the branches. That is, for each branch you have to decide where the history should cease and create a tag named **grafts/<*branch-name*>** with the previous information.

Step 2: Create a clone

The following steps change the repository contents permanently. Since we want to continue using the existing repository as an archive, we need to create a clone. Also, it will once again be a bare repository, as it will be used for the **push** command.

```
> cd ..

> git clone --bare project.git temp-project.git
```

Step 3: Alter the history with the grafts file

Now you can prune the history in the cloned repository. For this, you need to create an **info/grafts** file and edit it. The **info/grafts** file has a simple format. Each line manipulates the predecessor relationship of a commit. For this, only the hash of the commit to manipulate will be written, followed by a space and then the hash of the new predecessor. If the second value is omitted, then the commit will have no predecessor.

In our example, commit **C** will have no predecessors. The following command creates a new **grafts** file and writes the hash of commit **C** into it:

```
> cd temp-project.git

> echo 166a7e047a85b318720dc6e857a5321f9a3df7b4 >info/grafts
```

If you are editing multiple branches, you need to add one line for every branch.

To check if the manipulation worked, you can use the **log** command. In our example, only commit **C** should appear.

```
> git log --pretty=oneline

166a7e047a85b318720dc6e857a5321f9a3df7b4 C
```

Step 4: Change the repository permanently

After the repository has been adjusted by using the **grafts** file, you can now create a permanent new commit history with the **filter-branch** command. This command takes all commits in the specified branch and creates new commits according to the specified filter. In this particular case, you do not need to change the filter as the only objective is to change the commit history according to the **grafts** file.

Only the **--tag-name-filter** parameter is used, to bind the existing tags to the new commits.

```
> git filter-branch --tag-name-filter cat ---all

Rewrite 166a7e047a85b318720dc6e857a5321f9a3df7b4 (2/2)
Ref 'refs/heads/master' was rewritten
Ref 'refs/tags/grafts/master' was rewritten
WARNING: Ref 'refs/tags/release-1' is unchanged
Ref 'refs/tags/release-2' was rewritten
grafts/master -> grafts/master
```

```
        (166a7e047a85b318720dc6e857a5321f9a3df7b4
   -> 259ee224ac1f2d73898ec2ed25ad4dccd3c40f70)
release-1 -> release-1
        (577b8e2cf613c43ed969453477fadc189482c1fb
   -> 577b8e2cf613c43ed969453477fadc189482c1fb)
release-2 -> release-2 (166a7e047a85b318720dc6e857a5321f9a3df7b4
   -> 259ee224ac1f2d73898ec2ed25ad4dccd3c40f70)
```

The parameters used are as follows.

--tag-name-filter cat: All tags are newly created and point to the new commits.
-all: All branches in the repository are filtered.

You can see in the output of the **filter-branch** command that commit **C** was copied with hash **166a7** and has been assigned a new hash **259ee**.

In the output you can also see a warning. There is a **release-1** tag with no matching commit anymore in the new history. In our example, the **release-1** tag shows on commit **A**. However, after the changes, this is no longer part of the history.

These tags must be manually deleted, because otherwise they will ultimately prevent Git from deleting the corresponding old commits.

```
> git tag -d release-1
```

Step 5: Reduce the repository

At this stage, the repository is completely converted to the new history. However, the **filter-branch** command does not delete the old commits, as they are still referenced by other names. That is why the new repository is not smaller than the original.

With repeated cloning, however, you can create a new repository that only contains the new history. After that, you can delete the temporary repository.

```
> git clone --bare temp-project.git new-project.git
```

```
> rm -rf temp-project.git
```

The new repository can be compressed by using the **gc** command. This command does various cleanups in the repository. Among others, it compresses new files and deletes referenced objects that can no longer be retrieved.

```
> cd new-project.git

> git gc --prune
```

The **--prune** option indicates that all file versions that are no longer needed must be removed.

You can now notify all developers that a new repository is available and can be cloned.

Linking the Archive Repository

If you want to access historical information, the current repository must be linked with the archive repository. This is only a local link in the developer repository and can be activated individually by each developer.

For the following procedure, we assume that a developer already has his or her own clone (new project directory) of the new repository. In this repository, there is already a new commit **D** (See the bottom section of Figure 22.1).

Step 1: Clone the archive repository

To access the historical information, you will need a clone of the archive repository. Since there is no development in the archive repository, a bare clone is good enough.

```
> git clone --bare project.git archive-project.git
```

Step 2: Link the archive repository

The commits in the archive repository must be made available in the developer repository.

In order for a repository to access the commits of some other repository, "alternate" paths can be specified in the **.git/objects/info/alternates** file. Each line in this file specifies the absolute path to the **objects** directory of another repository.

Note that you must specify the actual path to the **objects** directory. The path to the project's root directory is not enough.

Use the **echo** command to add a new line to the **alternates** file.

```
> cd new-project

> echo /gitrepos/archive-project.git/objects

>> .git/objects/info/alternates
```

Step 3: Connect to the histories

Finally, using the already familiar **.git/info/grafts** file, commit **C'** must be linked to commit **B** in the archive repository.

In this case, the prepared **grafts** tag will be very helpful as it contains all the necessary information (See Step 1 in the previous sequence).

```
> git show grafts/master --pretty=oneline

tag grafts/master
Predecessor: dcbddd5cd590de3d30e1ecca1882c9187e7eab95
259ee224ac1f2d73898ec2ed25ad4dccd3c40f70 C
diff --git a/foo.txt b/foo.txt
..
```

You can see two commit hashes in the output. The first, **dcbdd**, corresponds to the historically correct predecessor, commit **B**. The second hash, **259ee**, corresponds to the new commit **C** in the current repository.

In the **grafts** file the hashes must be specified in reverse order. First comes commit **C'**, followed by a space and the new predecessor, commit **B**.

```
> echo 259ee224ac1f2d73898ec2ed25ad4dccd3c40f70 \
       dcbddd5cd590de3d30e1ecca1882c9187e7eab95 \
       >.git/info/grafts
```

To verify that the command terminated successfully, use the **log** command. The output must now contain commits **A** and **B**.

```
> git log --pretty=oneline

da8ba94d6bd9ec293f22a558756a91927f8b3525 D
259ee224ac1f2d73898ec2ed25ad4dccd3c40f70 C
dcbddd5cd590de3d30e1ecca1882c9187e7eab95 B
577b8e2cf613c43ed969453477fadc189482c1fb A
```

All historical information is now available In the current development repository.

Why Not the Alternatives?

Why Not Fetch the Archive Repository?

The workflow described uses the **objects/info/alternates** file to link the commits in a repository. An alternative is to use the normal **fetch** command to import these commits. The use of the **grafts** file to create the parent relationship would work anyway.

However, the workflow assumes that access to the history is only required rarely and temporarily. In this case, the solution with the **alternates** file is more useful because its own repository is not increased by more commits.

Chapter 23
Using Other Version Controls in Parallel

In many businesses and organizations, the tool for the versioning and the related processes is managed centrally. Individual projects and teams cannot just use a different version control system such as Git. The enterprise-wide migration to Git requires feasibility studies, strategic decisions, migration plans, etc. --so much time.

Despite everything, it is possible to use some skills of Git in the local development environment and synchronize the results with the central versioning.

For a local use Git provides the following advantages:

- Even if there is no access to the central versioning, local commits are possible.
- Fine-grained commits, also of intermediate objects, can be performed. The versioning is used as a safety net during development.
- Local branches for prototypes and feature-based work are possible.
- The good merge and rebasing support in Git can be useful.

This workflow shows how a local Git repository can work together with a central versioning so that

- changes in the central versioning can be imported into the local repository and

- local changes can be transferred to the central versioning.

For interconnectivity with Subversion, there is the **git-svn** command so this workflow is not required.

Overview

To describe the collaboration of Git and a central versioning, we use CVS. The basic sequence works the same for other central version controls.

Figure 23.1 shows a CVS server and repositories on the developer computer.

The developer has two local Git repositories. A “sync repository,” which is used to synchronize with the central version, and a “work repository,” in which the actual development takes place.

The sync repository is connected to the central version control (CVS-directories) and includes Git objects (in the **.git** directory). The central versioning is configured (through the **.cvsignore** file) such that Git objects are ignored. Git is configured (through the **.gitignore** file) so that CVS metadata is ignored.

First, files that have changed in the central version control are recorded in the sync repository (**cvs update**). Then a new Git commit is created on the **cvs** branch. This is then imported to the work repository (**fetch** command) and then merged with the **master** branch using the **merge** command.

In order to apply changes local to the **master** branch to the central versioning, the new commits on the **master** branch are transferred to the sync repository (with the **push** command). In the sync repository, the **master** branch is merged with the **cvs** branch. After that, the changes are saved in the central version control (with **cvs commit**).

Requirements

Optimistic locking: The central version management must support optimistic locking, i.e., files can be changed without acquiring locks.

Ignoring files and directories: The central versioning can exclude files and directories.

Flexibility of the project directory: The development tools (e.g. the build tools) do not require that the project be stored in exactly one place in the file system.

Workflow “Working with Other Version Controls in Parallel”

The company or team uses a centralized version control system. Individual developers are working with Git and synchronizing changes with the central system.

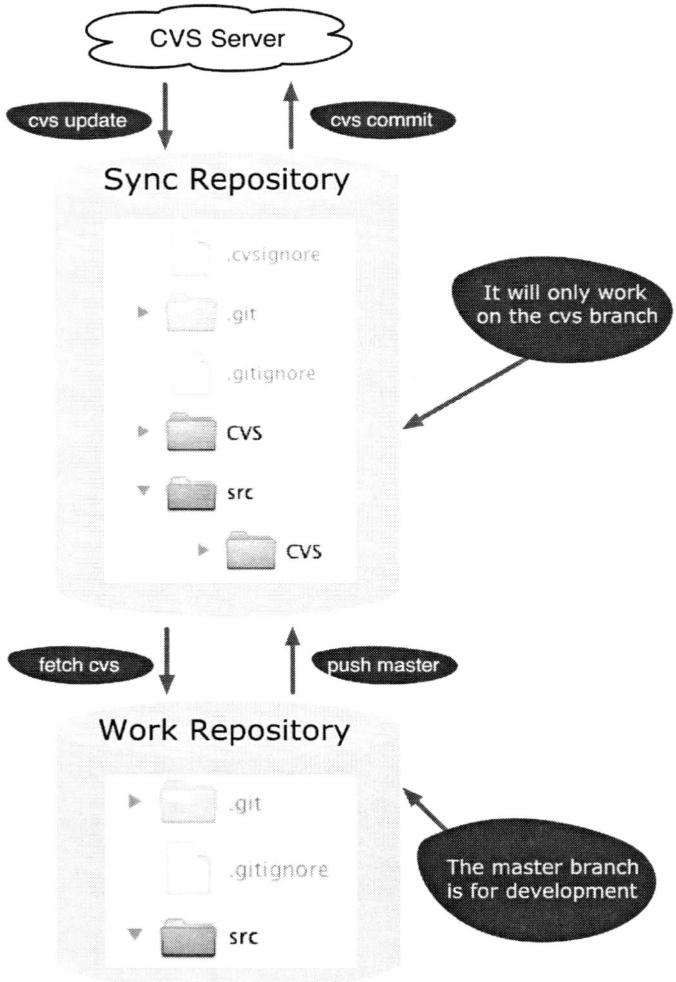

Figure 23.1: Workflow overview

Process and Implementation

You need the following information from your central versioning:

- How will the sources be brought initially from your version control? - **cvs checkout**
- Where and how is meta information stored in the file system? - **CVS directories**
- How do you exclude files in Subversion? - .**cvsignore** file
- How will updates be fetched from the central versioning? - **cvs update**
- How will files be added to your new versioning? - **cvs add**
- How will changes be transmitted to the central versioning? – **cvs commit**

Initial Setup of the Repository

The following steps show how the sync repository and the work repository are set up initially. The starting point is an existing local CVS project (**cvsproject**), which was created with **cvs checkout**.

Step 1: Create new sync repository

First, a new Git repository is initialized in the CVS project directory.

```
> cd cvsproject
```

```
> git init
```

Step 2: Configure the .gitignore file

All files, except the CVS metafiles, should be imported to the sync repository. Therefore, the **CVS** directory has to be listed in the **.gitignore** file.

```
> echo CVS/ > .gitignore
```

The **echo** command creates a new **.gitignore** file containing the content of **CVS/**.

Step 3: Configure the .cvsignore file

Git's meta information is not versioned in the central versioning. So you have to exclude the **.git** directory and the **.gitignore** file. In CVS this works by adding the directory and file to the **.cvsignore** file.

```
> echo .git >> .cvsignore
```

```
> echo .gitignore >> .cvsignore
```

If the **.cvsignore** file previously does not exist, it will be created automatically and must be added to the CVS repository with **cvs add**.

```
> cvs add .cvsignore
```

Then, you send the changes to CVS-Server with **cvs commit**.

```
> cvs commit
```

Step 4: Add files to sync repository

Now that all preparation has been completed, the project files can be added to the sync repository.

```
> git add .
```

Attention! Version control systems, including Git, have the habit of adapting the end of line characters in text files (LF or CRLF). If the central version control and Git handle line endings differently, you can disable changing line endings in Git: **git config core.autocrlf false**.

Some central version control systems, including Subversion, utilize a global revision number. In this case, it helps to include this revision number in the Git commit comment. This revision number can be tracked very easily and can reveal which progress had been imported. Unfortunately, CVS does not have such a revision number.

```
> git commit -m "Initial import of CVS"
```

Step 5: Create a cvs branch in the sync repository

The sync repository will work in the future on a separate **cvs** branch. This branch has yet to be created and activated.

```
> git checkout -b cvs
```

Step 6: Create a work repository

The work repository is created as a clone of the sync repository. When you create the clone, the **master** branch is set as the active branch automatically.

```
> cd ..
```

```
> git clone cvsproject gitproject
```

With this step, the initial preparation is complete.

Bringing Changes from the Central Version Control

This section describes how innovations from the centralized version control are brought from the sync repository to the work repository.

Step 1: Transfer the modified files into thesync repository

The workspace of the sync repository contains the necessary meta-information for comparison with the central versioning. Therefore, you can obtain changes from the CVS server through this workspace.

```
> cd cvsproject
```

```
> cvs update
```

Here, the **cvs update** command can never cause CVS conflicts. In the **cvs** branch of the sync repository there is always a “clean” old version of the central versioning

Subsequently, changes that have been made through CVS in the sync workspace are compiled using the **add** command to a Git commit. Then the commit is finished.

```
> git add --all .
```

The **--all** parameter adds new and edited files to the commit and simultaneously removes the deleted files.

```
> git commit -m "Changes from CVS"
```

Step 2: Commit changes to the work repository

So far, the commit with the CVS changes only exists in the sync repository. Since the work repository is a clone of the sync repository, the remote entry (**origin**) is automatically there too. With the **fetch** command, you can import the new commit with CVS changes to the work repository.

```
> cd gitproject
```

```
> git fetch origin
```

Step 3: Apply changes to the master branch

At this stage, the changes are only available on the **cvs** branch and not on the **master** branch. The final step consists of a **merge** command. Therefore, this can lead to conflicts if there were parallel changes to the same files in CVS and the local Git. The normal Git tools can be used to clean up the conflicts (see Figure 23.2).

```
> git merge origin/cvs
```

After these steps, the current version from the central versioning, which has been merged with the local changes, can be found in the work repository.

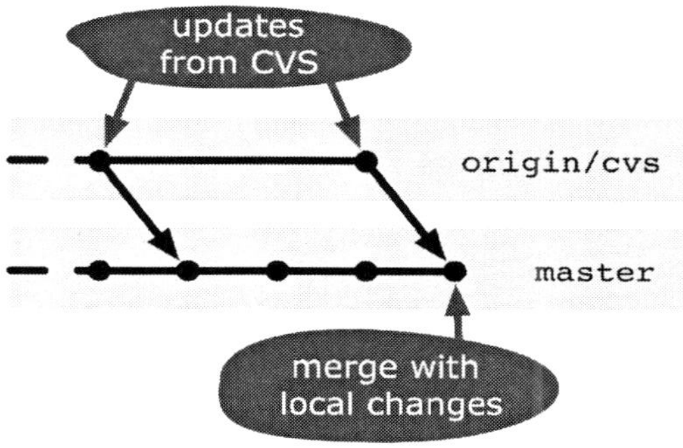

Figure 23.2: Copying CVS updates to the master branch

Transferring Changes to the Central Version Control

This section explains how to transfer changes from the work repository to the central version management via the sync repository.

Step 1: Get the latest version from the centralized version control

Before the local changes are transferred to the central version management, the latest changes should always be taken out of the center. To do this, follow the steps from the previous section.

By upgrading, the probability of conflicts is minimized during the subsequent transfer of your own changes to the central versioning. In addition, you can test again if the changes you have made will work with the latest central version.

The local changes on the **master** branch must be transferred to the sync repository. Since the sync repository was registered with the remote cloning as “origin”, a simple **push** command will do.

```
> cd gitproject

> git push
```

Step 3: Accept changes on the cvs branch

The new commits and updated files are located in the sync repository in the **master** branch. To apply these changes to the central version control, a merge to the **cvs** branch is still necessary. This will not cause any conflicts since the **cvs** branch has no changes (see Figure 23.3).

```
> cd cvsproject

> git merge --no-commit --no-ff master
```

The parameters used in the **merge** command are as follows.

--no-commit: Since there can still be conflicts in the subsequent CVS commit, the Git merge is first performed without a final commit.
--no-ff: This option prevents Git fast-forward merges.

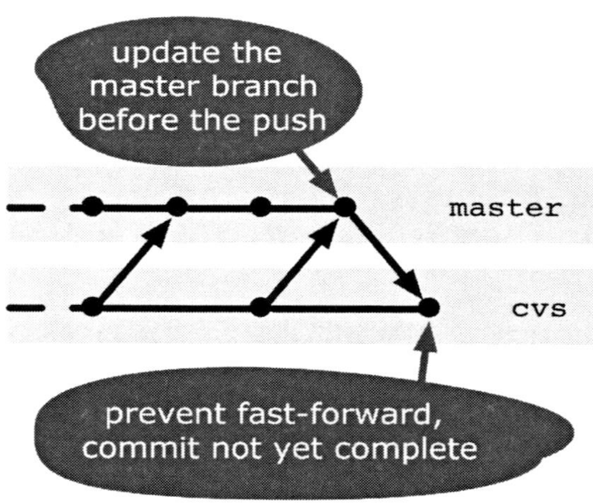

Figure 23.3: Preparing the CVS commit in the cvs branch

Step 4: Transferring changes to the central version control

The local changes can now be transferred to the central version management. Depending on whether there are new files, deleted files or changed files, the necessary commands are run on the central version control, e.g. **cvs commit** if there were only changed files:

```
> cvs commit
```

If there is a conflict during the cvs commit, then there must have been changes since the last **cvs update** changes that compete with the local changes. In this case, you have to reset the current merge attempt—the open commit.

```
> git reset --hard HEAD
```

Then, you can start again at Step 1 to fetch the last competing changes from the central version control and merge them with the **master** branch.

When you have successfully transferred the changes to the central version control, proceed to the next step.

Step 5: Get updates from the central version control

Some version control systems change files when doing a commit or at the first update after a commit. So you can, for example, get CVS to use the current version number or the history of changes in the head of a file (keyword substitution). Therefore, again it is important to fetch the files from the centralized version control after a successful CVS commit.

```
> cvs update
```

Step 6: Perform a commit to the cvs branch

Now it is time to close the open merge commit. Before you do that, add any possible CVS substitutions to the merge commit with the **add** command:

```
> git add .
> git commit -m "Changes from Git recorded"
```

Step 7: Update the master branch in the work repository

After the previous step there is now a new commit on the cvs **branch** in the sync repository. Before further work, the **cvs** branch must be with the **master** branch in the work repository. To this end, the commit is transferred to the work repository first.

```
> cd gitproject
> git fetch origin
```

Next, do a merge. This merge is always a fast-forward merge, as there should be no interim changes on the **master** branch.

```
> git merge origin/cvs
```

After these steps, any local changes in the central version control are included. In the work repository there is a version that corresponds to the current version of the central versioning. Figure 23.4 shows all the commits and branches as they are created by the procedure described.

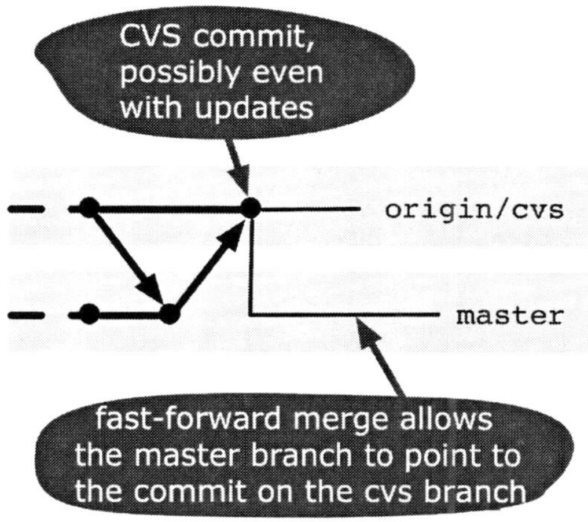

Figure 23.4: Commits and branches after the transfer

Why Not the Alternatives?

Why Not Just One Repository?

The sequence in this workflow also works with just one Git repository, i.e., you can have the local development in the sync repository instead. You then switch between the **cvs** branch and the **master** branch, depending on whether you are synchronizing or developing. However, experience has shown that it is difficult to keep track of where and what actions need to be performed.

It often happens that, especially when you are synchronizing, commands are executed on the wrong branch.

Another problem can arise if the meta-information of the central versioning is accidentally deleted during development, for example if you delete the whole CVS directory when refactoring.

Chapter 24
Migrating to Git

To successfully migrate from another version management to Git, it takes more than just a transfer of software versions to a Git repository. This workflow shows how to organize the migration of a project and what you should bear in mind:

- Knowledge structure and know-how transfer
- Strategic decisions you should take
- Transfer of content to a Git repository
- Expiration of the actual migration
- Dragging changes that have arisen since the creation of the Git repository in the old version management

Overview

The migration process is divided into several phases. If several projects need to be migrated in succession, some of these phases can be skipped.

1. Learn Git, gain experience
2. Make decisions
3. Find branches
4. Prepare the repository
5. Fetch branches
6. Take the repository in question
7. Clean up

Requirements

The project is taken from another version control system. We have also made the following assumptions:

Permissions: You should have free write access to all the files and directories in the workspace. In particular, the files may not be set to "Read only." Optionally, the configuration of the old version management needs to be adapted.

Ignoring directories: The Git repository is created in the workspace of the other version management. A **.git** directory that is ignored in the old version management must be able to protect it from accidental deletion.

Attention! Unlike most of the previous workflows, this workflow is highly dependent on external factors: What version control is used? How are the projects organized? How are branches used? You will probably not implement this workflow exactly as it is described here. So plan a little time to adjust the workflow to your requirements.

Workflow "Migrating to Git"

A project from another version control system is migrated to Git. All software versions to be further developed are adopted in the Git repository. Afterward, you can continue working with the new repository. If required, "trickling" changes from the old version management need to be tightened.

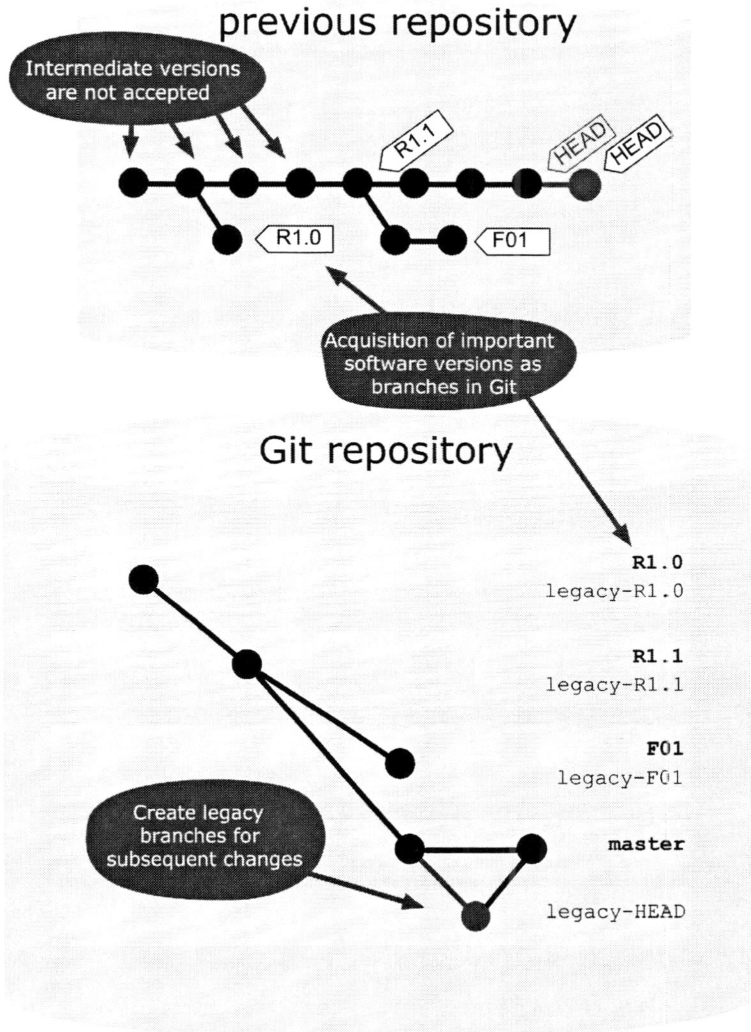

Figure 24.1: Workflow overview

Process and Implementation

Learn Git, Gain Experience

Git is not difficult to learn, because the basic concepts are logical and well thought of (which hopefully we have been able to convince you with this book). For developers who have worked a lot with centralized version control systems, some aspects of Git need to be gotten used to, including working with remote repositories or dealing with branches. Therefore, we recommend that one or two developers prepare to support the team as a coach during migration.

Step 1: Test Git

Start a little unimportant sample project. It is best to choose something that is not yet in the old version control. Perhaps if you want to develop just a new utility class, try a new Java library or write some shell scripts for server management.

Start with the Git command line, even if you later use a Git front-end or a plug-in for your development. So, first learn Git "unfiltered." Although the front end is much easier, it often disguises what really happens in Git. When it comes to problems with the migration, at least you should know what is going on behind the scenes. Try basic commands such as **add**, **commit**, **push**, **pull** and **log**.

After that you should look at branches, because that is the area where most difficulties are initially located. Try the workflows "Developing on the Same Branch" and "Developing with Feature Branches." Create a few conflicts on purpose to practice the conflict resolution.

Then you can try the front-end. There is now a good selection. Try those variants that match your development environment and target platform. Pay special attention to how well the merge conflict resolution is supported. At this point, the environments differ significantly.

As a coach, you should at least master the following items:

- You have gained so much experience that you can teach your colleagues basic Git commands such as **add**, **commit**, **status**, **diff**, **log**, **push** and **pull**.
- You should look at the following commands closely because they operate differently from their counterparts in traditional version control systems: **branch**, **checkout**, **reset**, **merge** and **rebase**.
- You have worked with at least one of the two branching strategies: "Developing on the Same Branch" and "Developing with Feature Branches."
- You can set up Git and possibly a front-end on a developer machine.
- You can resolve merge conflicts (possibly also on the front-end).

Step 2 (Optional): Work in parallel in the other version control

You can also learn Git by putting it to use in parallel with the old version control for a while, so while you are developing locally with Git, the project remains in the central versioning. See the workflow "Using Other Version Control Systems in Parallel ."

Make Decisions

A few important decisions should be made early.

Step 1: Migrate all projects at once?

This workflow describes how to migrate a project. If you have multiple projects, you can perform this workflow several times in succession. However, you can also carry out migration for all the projects in parallel. This has both advantages and disadvantages compared to a single project migration.

Advantages

- You can use Git extensively earlier.
- You benefit sooner from the advantages of Git .
- After the migration you only need to support one version control system.

Disadvantages

- The know-how transfer becomes more difficult. In the first two to three weeks after the migration, many questions will be asked. If there are many developers, and only one coach who is familiar with Git, this can jeopardize the success of the migration.
- Problems with migration can easily cause major issues, when many projects are affected at the same time.
- If in the initial phase you make a decision that later turns out to be unfavorable, this must be corrected in many projects.

Our recommendation: If you are not sure, we recommend you start with a single project in order to determine how you will proceed.

Step 2: Which projects should be migrated?

We cannot help you with this decision.

Step 3: Should the existing structure be adopted?

How are your projects currently organized?

- Are all projects in the same repository? Or are they in different repositories?

- Do the projects have a common release cycle? Are they even part of the same product?
- Are there common cross-project changes?
- Are the projects more closely or loosely coupled?

Unfortunately, we cannot say what the ideal Git repository structure for your projects should look like. We can only give you some rough rules of thumb:

- If you currently store all your projects in a repository, we tend to suggest you do the same in Git.
- If the projects have a common release cycle, then we would suggest a common repository in Git because then the workflow “Performing A Release” can be applied across the project.
- Even frequent cross-project changes are an indicator for a shared repository.
- If the projects are loosely coupled, this might be a candidate for separate repositories.
- Git is not suitable for binary files or resources that are large or change often. You can use Git to manage such files, but they are better stored in a separate repository, so that the performance of the normal (source code) projects does not suffer.

Our recommendation: If in doubt, just start with a structure similar to the structure in your previous version management. Later you can create a better structure using the “Merging Small Projects” and “Splitting A Large Project” workflows.

Step 4: Can you afford development interruption during the migration?

If yes, this simplifies the migration process a little. Make the new repository ready and retire the old repository. The developers should then switch over to Git and do a release from Git.

However, if you operate a 24/7 system, you might want to hold any hotfixes from the old version management as long as possible during migration, until the developers are able to provide release versions from the Git repository. In this case, you have to deal with how you can monitor changes from the old repository.

Step 5: Which branching strategy do you want to use?

"Developing on the Same Branch" or "Developing with Feature Branches"? You should decide on this in time so that you can give the developers the new workflow before migration, so that afterwards you can continue working equally productively.

Our recommendation: If you are not sure, start with "Developing on the Same Branch" because the classic version management is similar.

Step 6: Which front-end do you want to use?

Finally, you should supply the developers with the right software before the migration.

Find Branches

Next, you need to find out which software releases in the old repository are to be developed as Git branches:

- The main line of development, known in other version control systems as trunk or main line, is to be fetched safely.
- Each version, for which bug fixes or extensions must be supplied, should be fetched as a branch in Git. If you develop a product that is installed at the customer site, there could be many versions. If you are developing a web application, however, you may only be using two branches: one for the productive version, on which

hotfixes are built, and one for the feature development for the next release.

- If you work with feature-branches in your previous version control, you should also use this in Git or finish and close the branches just before the migration. The latter makes migration easier, of course.

In many version control systems, there are the so-called floating tags, which are tags like **RELEASE3**, which can be moved to hotfixes. Such tags are often candidates for release branches in Git.

The fewer branches you have to take, the less work you have to do at the migration. So choose wisely what you really need, and think when you will perform the migration. Maybe there is a point in time where a few branches should be taken from the old version control.

Subsequently, draw a “relationship” diagram for all the branches found. In the simplest case, this is a sequence with the oldest version at the bottom and the latest at the top.

Prepare the Repository

Next, create the Git repository. So that you can set it up thoroughly and test it, you should allow a few days (or weeks) before starting the actual migration. However, in the meantime, this means new changes in the old repository. Therefore, it will be necessary to monitor these changes later.

To achieve this, you can work on the Git part with two branches, one represents the development in Git and the other the development in the old repository. We call the latter the legacy branch. We do not develop on the legacy branch, it is only for software versions from the old repository. Transfer these changes later with a merge on the development branch.

If the concept of legacy branches somehow reminds you of remote-tracking branches, then you have just recognized a pattern. Both illustrate operations from another repository into the local repository.

In this example we use the following naming convention: For branches or tags from the old version management, we use capital letters, e.g. **RELEASE3**. In Git we use lowercase letters and call the development branch **release3** and the legacy branch **legacy-release3**.

Step 1: Get the project from the old version management

A workspace that includes project files is obtained from the old version control. In other version control systems it is often called a checkout.

Step 2: Create a Git repository

In this workspace from the old version control, a Git repository is now created. The result is a workspace that is associated with both version control systems. We call this a dual-use workspace.

```
> cd old-vcs-workspace
> git init
```

Step 3: Create a local backup

When you are working with two different version control systems at the same time, it may well happen that you specify a force or a clean in the wrong place. Therefore, a backup is not a bad idea:

```
> git clone --no-hardlinks --bare . /backups/myproject.git
> git remote add backup /backups/myproject.git
```

Later, you should secure it occasionally.

```
> git push --all backup
```

To restore, clone the repository into a temporary directory, then switch to the desired Git branch and move the **.git** directory in the workspace of the old version control.

Step 4: Allow to ignore metafiles

First, ensure that the two version control systems do not hit each other's workspace.

The metafiles of the old version control should not be taken into the Git repository. For this, create a **.gitignore** file and enter the paths or file patterns to be ignored. The **status** command may no longer show the metafiles from the old version management.

```
> git commit .gitignore -m "ignore legacy metafiles"
```

Conversely, the old version management must be configured so that the **.git** directory and the **.gitignore** file are preserved. For instance, in CVS you can do this by creating a **.cvsignore** file in the user directory.

Fetch the Branches

To fetch the tags and branches from the old version control, there are steps to execute. You start with the oldest branch or tag that is to be fetched.

Step 1: If necessary, switch to the previous branch

With the first branch, you can skip this step because there is no predecessor branch.

In Figure 24.1, you can see which is the predecessor of a branch. If you want to migrate **RELEASE3**, then switch now to its predecessor, i.e. to the legacy branch for **RELEASE2**.

```
> git checkout legacy-release2
```

Step 2: Create a legacy branch

Create a legacy branch for the version. For example, for **RELEASE3** you would create

```
> git branch legacy-release3
```

Step 3: Take the version from the old version management

Now, we switch to the old version management at the software version we want to take, e.g. **RELEASE3**.

```
> git status
```

The **status** command shows what changes from **RELEASE2** are on **RELEASE3**. You should consider briefly whether it looks plausible. If so, you can accept the changes in the new legacy branch.

```
> git add --all
> git commit -m "RELEASE3 retrieved from legacy-cvs"
```

Step 4: Leave generated files unversioned

The current software version is built and tested. This probably creates new files that should not be included in the repository. You must create a **.gitignore** file.

```
> git commit .gitignore -m "ignore build artifacts"
```

Step 5: Create a Git branch

Now create a Git branch on which development will later take place.

```
> git branch release3
```

Step 6: Check the result

You should check the result again. So that the metadata of the version control systems do not interfere with the process, comparison should be performed in temporary directories outside the workspace. The **archive** command can help. This command exports the file tree of all commits to an archive file (tar or zip). The current version of the branch in Git, in this case **release3**, is written to a temporary directory named **git-vcs**.

```
> git archive release3 | tar -x -C /tmp/git-vcs
```

Next, export the version from the old version management, for example to **/tmp/legacy-vcs**. Now you can make a comparison, for example, with **kdiff3**. Except for the **.gitignore** file, there should be no differences.

```
> kdiff3 /tmp/git-vcs/ /tmp/legacy-vcs
```

Take the repository in question

Our goal is to provide a transition that is as friction-free as possible.

Step 1: Announcement

Announce the migration on time. The notice should contain the following information:

Introduction: Invite everybody to a meeting in which the normal work with Git is shown.

Installing the development environment: Briefly describe how to set up the development environment (Git and IDE plug-ins to install and configure), and how you can clone a project.

Freeze time: Encourage employees to bring any local changes in the old version control to a pre-determined date and from then reload any new changes.

Resume date: When can people resume work with the new Git repository?

Emergency plan: Hotfix releases can also be carried out during the transition phase from the old version management. The changes must then be tightened later in Git. It is important to clearly acknowledge that this has to be made essential. Otherwise, an already fixed bug could be delivered again at a Git release.

Step 2: Introduction

Now show them how to work with Git. For day to day operations, you only need a few commands. You can, for example, introduce the workflow "Developing on the Same Branch". For demonstration you can just use a clone of the new repository. You can experiment to your heart's content and then just throw away the clone.

Step 3: Get the recent changes

After the freeze point, you have to follow all the changes from the old repository since the creation of the Git repositories. This is done in the dual-use workspace for each legacy branch. You first switch to the legacy branch in Git.

```
> git checkout legacy-release3
```

Then you switch to the old version management on the appropriate branch or tag, e.g. **RELEASE3**, and check if there have been any changes.

```
> git status
```

If there have been no changes, you are covered in the legacy branch.

```
> git add -all
```

```
> git commit -m "updating legacy-release3 from old vcs"
```

Thereafter, the changes in the new branch can be fetched for further development in Git.

```
> git checkout
```

```
> git merge legacy-release3
```

If no development has taken place in Git, there will be no merge conflict here.

In this way, you can trace if the development has already begun in Git, if a developer has missed the freeze date, or if a hotfix piece had to be carried out in the old version management. In such a case, however, there may be merge conflicts that you must resolve manually.

Step 4: Publish the new repository

After all branches have been traced, you can put the repository on the server. Then, add the known URL and ask the developer to clone the repository and proceed with development (Continue time).

Step 5: Build the product or perform a release

Now comes the time to build the current version of your product to ensure that you can now do a release without the old version management.

Step 6: Make the old repository read-only

As soon as you are able to perform a new release (or build a product) from the new repository, you should make the old repository read-only. It is then only used as an archive for the history of the project.

Step 7: Support the developers

Do not forget to make time to support the developers during the first few weeks. In particular, you should be prepared to resolve merge conflicts and make local edits, such as by using the **reset** command or by using interactive rebasing.

Clean up

After the old repository has been disconnected, you can delete the legacy branches. The best way to do is in a freshly cloned workspace and not in the dual-use workspace, because there is no linked origin in a fresh clone.

```
> git branch -d legacy-release3
> git push origin :legacy-release3
```

Why Not the Alternatives?

Why Not Take over the Whole History?

In this workflow, only individual software versions that are to be developed further are taken. This has the disadvantage that you cannot see the old history in the new Git repository. The history remains in the old repository.

There are various tools (from Git as well as from independent projects) for acquiring a history. For example, the **cvsimport** command can transfer CVS repository contents to a Git repository. However, since the structure in the CVS repository is very different than that in Git, the translation is not trivial and the quality of the result may vary depending on the manner in which CVS was used previously. In any case, you should look at the import result very carefully before you continue working with it. You may have to rework it to make it fit.

It is the thing that has prevented us from going this route. Secondly, we wanted to show that a migration path was feasible, regardless of which version control system you are migrating from.

Can We Get Rid of the Legacy Branches?

In the workflow legacy branches are initially created that reflect the current states of branches and tags in the old version management. At the end of the workflow, these legacy branches will be deleted. They serve only one purpose: namely, the fetching of subsequent changes from the old repository. If you can interrupt the development for a few days (for example, when the team is attending a training course or can work on something else), then you can certainly do without legacy branches and simplify the workflow a bit.

Can We Do without the Dual-Use Workspace?

In the dual-use workspace you can work with Git and the old version management at the same time. This facilitates the exchange of software versions: After getting the desired version, you can perform a commit in Git.

However, a dual-use workspace is not always possible with any version control system. In such cases where it is not possible, you could operate with two separate workspaces. Then you would have to change back and forth, possibly by using a shell script or rsync. So, eliminating the dual-use workspace is possible, but it would make migration much more complex.

Chapter 25 What Else Is There?

In this book we have limited ourselves to the Git concepts and commands that are used in typical project situations in business. The following chapter gives you an overview of what else is there in Git. The commands are not described in detail, but only so far as is necessary for you to grasp the concepts.

Interactive Rebasing—Making the History Better

We have mentioned rebasing many times in this book. It is used to apply changes in commits again and produce new commits, for example if you want to replant a branch.

If you put a lot of emphasis on the commit history, then you can use rebasing to summarize (**squash** command), split (**edit** command) or re-sort commits. For this, you call the **rebase** command with the **--interactive** parameter. The commit from which the history is to be changed is given as the second parameter. For example, to change the last three commits, use the following command.

```
> git rebase --interactive HEAD~3
```

As a result, a text editor will show three commits.

```
pick 927d33a commit 3
pick 7d343d0 commit 4
pick fbe58cb commit 5
```

```
# Rebase 940d0db..fbe58cb onto 940d0db
#
# Commands:
# p, pick = use commit
# r, reword = use commit, but edit the commit message
# e, edit = use commit, but stop for amending
# s, squash = use commit, but meld into previous commit
# f, fixup = like "squash", but discard this commit's log message
# x, exec = run command (the rest of the line) using shell
#
# If you remove a line here THAT COMMIT WILL BE LOST.
# However, if you remove everything, the rebase will be aborted.
#
```

In the text file the commits can be rearranged or changed using the commands listed. After closing the editor Git will process the commits according to the commands.

Attention! The commit history should never be changed after executing the **push** command. Other team members may already been relying on the “old” commits.

Dealing with Patches

In the Unix world especially, changes are often transmitted via a patch file. In pure Git environments there seldom is a need to work directly with patches. Here changes are replaced by commits. If it is necessary to use patches, Git supports the creation and installation of patches.

Patches can be created with the **diff** command.

```
> git diff rel-1.0.0 HEAD >local.patch
```

To load the changes into another repository, use the **apply** command.

```
> git apply local.patch
```

```
> git commit -m "applied patch"
```

Sending Patches by Email

Git also allows you to send commits by patch-mail and import them to another repository. This is a substitute for **pull** and **push**. Information from the original commits (authors, dates) is retained. Commit hashes, however, are not.

The **format-patch** command creates a separate patch file in mbox format for each commit in the specified range. The mbox format is a text file for emails.

```
> git format-patch rel-1.0.0..HEAD
```

```
0001-a7.patch
0002-a8.patch
0003-a9.patch
0004-a9.patch
```

You can now send the files to yourself or use the Git **send-email** command.

```
> git send-email --to "mailto:rp@etosquare.de"
```

The recipient can import the emails with the **am** command to a repository. Here you can select the patches individually or specify all using the wildcard character.

```
> git am 0*.patch
```

Bundles—pull in Offline Mode

The two previous sections discussed transferring patches from one repository to another. If you want to transfer commits, you normally use the **pull** or **push** command. However, if there is no direct connection between the computers hosting the two repositories, you can create a bundle. A bundle contains commits and you can use the **fetch** or **pull** command against one.

As the first step, create a bundle using the **bundle-create** command. The bundle will contain all the commits to be transferred.

```
> git bundle create local.bundle rel-1.0.0..HEAD
```

The generated file can then be transferred to another computer by email or with a USB stick. There you can import the commits from the bundle to another repository. The commit hashes will be retained.

```
> git pull local.bundle HEAD
```

Creating An Archive

You can use the **archive** command to export the contents of a project as an archive without exporting the Git metadata (the **.git** directory). This command supports the tar and zip formats.

```
> git archive HEAD --format=tar > archive.tar
```

```
> git archive HEAD --format=zip > archive.zip
```

```
> git archive HEAD --format=tar | gzip > archive.tar.gz
```

You can also pack only individual subdirectories into an archive.

```
> git archive HEAD subdir --format=tar > archive.tar
```

You can also create an archive of a remote repository using the **--remote** parameter.

Graphical Tools for Git

In this book we have worked exclusively with the command line. However, Git also ships with two graphical tools. One of them is the Git GUI, which can create commits. You use the **gui** command to open it (See Figure 25.1).

```
> git gui
```

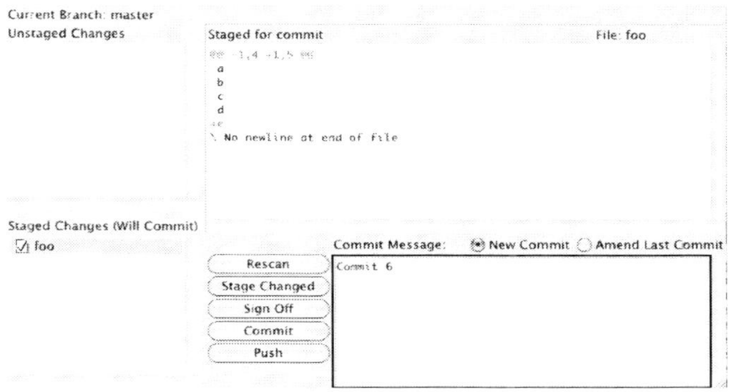

Figure 25.1: A graphical tool for creating commits

There is also GITK, another graphical tool you can open with the **gitk** command. This one can handle the history (See Figure 25.2).

```
> git gitk -all
```

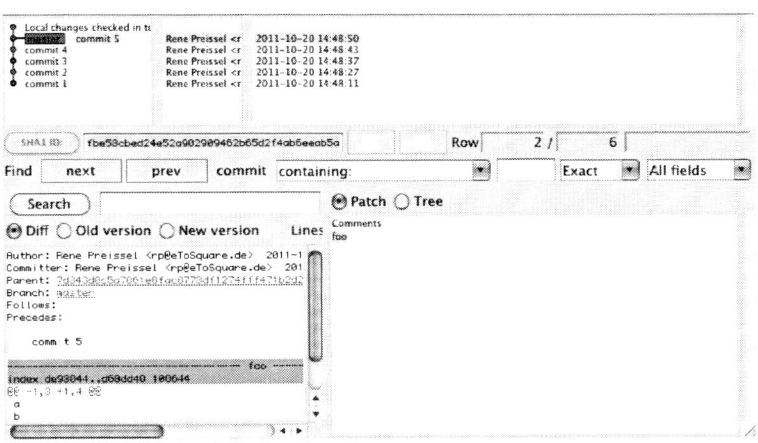

Figure 25.2: A graphical tool for viewing the history

Viewing A Repository with A Web BrowserGitWeb is a tool for viewing and searching a Git repository in the browser

(See Figure 25.3). GitWeb shows all the commits and branches in the repository. You can look at the files in a commit and examine the changes. With GitWeb you can also search for files and commits.

To start and stop GitWeb, use the **instaweb** command.

```
> git instaweb start
> git instaweb stop
```

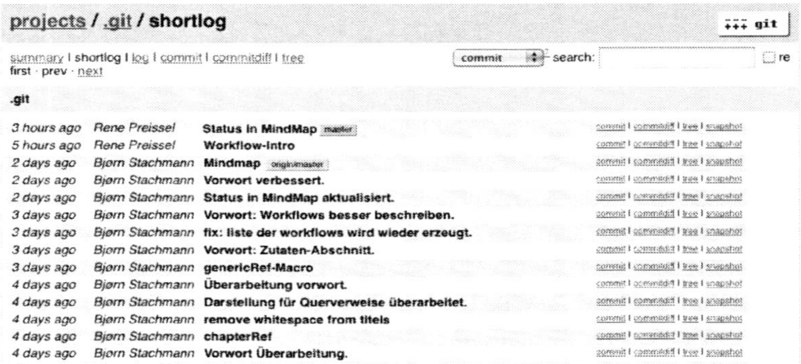

Figure 25.3: GitWeb

Working with Subversion

Git allows you to clone a Subversion repository (using the **svn-clone** command). The entire history will be imported. In the Git repository you can create local commits. You can always get the latest version from Subversion (using the **svn rebase** command). If the local commits need to be exported back to Subversion (using the **svn-dcommit** command), then a separate Subversion revision will be created for each commit.

```
> git svn clone http://localhost/projecta/trunk
> git svn rebase
> git svn dcommit
```

Command Aliases

Repeatedly typing Git commands with a long list of parameters can be quite tedious. With aliases you can minimize the amount of typing. Here you can configure global aliases for all the repositories on the computer or only for the current repository.

The global alias **ci**, short for **commit**, is defined as follows.

```
> git config --global alias.ci commit
```

A local alias **rema**, a shortcut to rebasing with the **master** branch, is defined as this.

```
> git config alias.rema 'rebase master'
```

Then you can use the aliases as normal commands.

```
> git ci
```

```
> git rema
```

Notes on Commits

Commits are immutable in Git. Although you can copy and change a commit, a new commit is later created. If you want to add a comment to a commit, you have notes at your disposal. Notes are mostly used by development tools to highlight commits.

The **notes add** command creates a new comment in a commit.

```
> git notes add -m "My Comment" HEAD
```

You can display the comment later with the **notes show** command.

```
> git notes show HEAD
```

Attention! Notes are not automatically transferred to another repository with a **pull** or a **push**. Unfortunately, there are no simple parameters for **notes** to achieve this. The following two commands show an example of how notes are transferred:

```
> git push origin refs/notes/*:refs/notes/*
> git fetch origin refs/notes/*:refs/notes/*
```

Extending Git with Hooks

You can create a hook to fire off certain scripts when a particular action occurs. For instance, it is possible to perform pre-determined checks before the actual commit, like if certain conventions have been adhered to in the commit comment (**commit-msg** hook).

Sample hooks are stored in the **.git/hooks** directory of each repository.

Hosting Repositories on GithubGithub (https://github.com) is a service provider for managing Git repositories and making them available on the Internet. Github offers SSH and HTTPS access to the repository.

Creating public repositories is free. For private repositories, you must use the paid version. Many open source projects are now using Github as a development center.

In particular, the pull workflow is well supported. You can clone an existing Github repository within Github. Server-side clones are called forks. You can work as usual on your own fork repository. You can create a local clone and changes are written back via the **push** command. If you want to transfer commit changes back to the source repository, you can send a pull request to the repository owner through Github. You can then pull and merge the changes using the **pull** command.

Chapter 26
Git's Shortcomings

In the previous chapters we have discussed the advantages of Git and how efficient it is to work with a distributed version control. This chapter deals with the problem areas of Git.

High Complexity

Dealing with a centralized version control is now standard knowledge of every developer. However, this is often limited to the basic functions, such as fetching new versions and uploading changes. Branching and repository administration are often carried out by build managers with specialist knowledge.

In Git, however, branching is a fundamental concept that must be understood with every commit, pull and push. Also, every developer is the administrator of his or her own repository. Every member of the team must also be able to deal with remotes and exchange between repositories.

In addition, compared to the centralized version control system, there is an extra push step after a commit in the normal flow in Git. While a commit is sufficient in a centralized version control system to make the changes visible, in Git the commit must still be transmitted with the push command to the central repository.

These are due to the complexity of a distributed version control and are also found in other distributed tools, such as

Mercurial. In all probability, software developers will have these concepts ready soon as standard knowledge.

In addition, Git also brings with it a few quirks. Originally, Git resides in the Linux kernel development. In Linux you must be used to working a lot with the command line. Git is powerful and there are a plethora of commands and parameters. If you look at the help pages of Git commands, you will almost feel killed by all the possibilities. The verbosity of the help pages is good to understand all the details, but they help little when it comes to distinguishing between the important and the unimportant.

Finally, a command name often highlights the technical aspect and not the application aspect. For example, the following command is used to discard local changes in Git:

```
> git checkout -- FILE
```

Got it?

Some Git command names also have a different meaning in other known version control systems. For example, in Subversion the command to discard local changes is as follows:

```
> svn revert FILE
```

A **revert** command is also available in Git, but it is for removing changes to an already conducted commit.

The point is Git is highly complex, and as such has a steep learning curve. Therefore, it is important that developers prepare well for the introduction of Git and it is important to define clear procedures for standard workflows.

For your effort, however, you will be rewarded with a very powerful tool that does not restrict you in your own way of working.

Complicated Submodules

The submodule concept was described in Chapter 11, "Dependencies between Repositories." Submodules are separate repositories that are linked from another repository (the main repository).

Cloning a repository with submodules is complicated and requires additional steps (the **submodule-init** and **submodule-update** commands). You can see clearly that the submodule concept was retrofitted.

With Git you can always restore a reproducible version of your project that includes submodules. Unfortunately, this also makes the work complicated. Changes to a submodule must first be completed with a separate commit. After that, the new commit of the submodule must be selected and subsequently persisted in the main repository with a second commit.

In many development projects, you always want the current versions of submodules integrated in the main project during the development phase. Git submodules do not support this approach. You must always select a commit explicitly.

The fact that submodules are stand-alone repositories, it is not possible to move files including the history between them.

This all makes people often omit submodules in Git. If technical modules serve only as a structuring unit within a project, then you would work best with a large repository in which all modules are included. So you can always have the latest versions of all modules and files including the history can be moved. However, separate release cycles, branches and tags for individual modules are not possible with this solution.

Alternatively, if the modules are not tightly coupled and require their own release cycles, then you can use an external component repository that supports dependency management (e.g. Maven or Ivy in Java) and use Git to version only the definitions of the dependencies of the modules (in Maven with the **pom.xml** file).

Resource Consumption for Large Binary Files

Git has a very efficient memory management. The content of a file is stored once only, even if there are multiple copies of the file. This also works across commit boundaries. That is, as long as the content of a file does not change, there is only one object for all Git commits.

In addition, Git objects are combined into packages and Git compresses them. This all leads to a very resource-efficient storage of files.

However, all versions of a file in the local repository are kept. As soon as you store large binary files in Git, like movies, photos, virtual machines, this will cause more resource consumption. When a new version of a large binary file is created, both the old and the new files are in the local repository.

In this case, centralized version control systems have the advantage that only the latest version of a binary file is available locally at the developer's machine. Older versions are only on the server.

As a consequence, you should try to minimize the number of large binary files in the actual Git development repository. "Small" binary files, such as Java libraries, are no problem for today's hard drives and network bandwidth.

If a repository becomes very large, you can delete the old versions of files using the workflow "Outsourcing Long Histories."

Repositories Can Only Be Dealt with in Its Entirety

In a commit Git always versions the entire project or directory. By contrast, most central versions administrations manage files individually. Therefore, central version controls also support partial checkouts, i.e., you can get individual subdirectories separately from a version.

In Git partial checkouts are not supported, since all the files are already available locally. The need for partial checkouts often indicates a lack of modularization in the project, i.e., you should create multiple repositories.

Often partial checkouts are used in central version controls to offset the slowness of the systems, a problem Git does not have.

If you really want to look at individual files only, then you can set up a GitWeb server (See the **instaweb** command). This allows direct access to certain files and versions.

Alternatively, you can use the **archive** command to export only parts of the repository.

Authorization Only on the Entire Repository

In the previous section we mentioned that a Git repository can only be dealt with in its entirety. This also applies to authorization.

With Git It is not possible to set up permissions for individual folders of a project. Either a user has full access to a repository, or he or she cannot access it. It is only possible to distinguish between read and write access, again only for the entire repository.

In open source projects the problem of different access permissions are often solved through the "Network of Trust" concept.

In "Network of Trust" none is allowed push access to the repository, it uses a pure pull workflow. In this workflow, developers generate local commits and send pull requests to integrators.

The integrators only accept pull requests from well known and trusted people. In other pull requests, the changes must first be verified by a trusted person. Git supports the distinction between author and committer and the concept of "signed commits." With signed commits a trusted committer signs to confirm that he has verified the changes. To this end, the commit message is extended accordingly:

```
Signed-off-by: Rene Preissel <rp@eToSquare.de>
```

With this, a new commit is created with the verified changes. The signing developer is written as the person who carried out the inspection.

Thus, in the "Network of Trust" the rigid assignment of rights for directories is replaced by a review process. In large open source projects (such as the Linux kernel), there are several levels of integrators. Only after several steps will a change end up in the official repository. The top level integrators does not have to control all commits, since they are already signed by trusted developers.

A modification of the "Network of Trust" workflow is supported by the tool Gerrit. All code changes need to go through a review process before the changes are accepted in the official branch.

For in-house projects, often neither fine-grained permissions for directories or complex formal review processes are necessary. All team members are allowed to see and modify all the files. Maximum release of a project or transition to a predefined test level should be limited. A developer can also be easily restricted by creating separate repositories with limited write access. Once a transition is about to happen, the commits of authorized users are transferred into another repository.

Moderate Graphical Tools for History Analysis

When it comes to merge conflicts in projects or problems after a merge error, then the commit history can be used to find the causes. It is often a question why a change was incorporated. With active development activities, and thus many commits and merges, that is not trivial.

Git offers a very powerful command line tools (**log**, **blame**, **annotate** commands) for analyzing the commit history. However, the graphical tool gitk that ships with Git and also the plug-ins for development environments (such as EGit) are not great. It is tedious to trace the paths. In this aspect, commercial version administration tools offer clearer display options.

Index